PLOTS

LEONARD HASTINGS SCHOFF MEMORIAL LECTURES

UNIVERSITY SEMINARS
LEONARD HASTINGS SCHOFF MEMORIAL LECTURES

The University Seminars at Columbia University sponsor an annual series of lectures, with the support of the Leonard Hastings Schoff and Suzanne Levick Schoff Memorial Fund. A member of the Columbia faculty is invited to deliver before a general audience three lectures on a topic of his or her choosing. Columbia University Press publishes the lectures.

David Cannadine, *The Rise and Fall of Class in Britain* 1993

Charles Larmore, *The Romantic Legacy* 1994

Saskia Sassen, *Losing Control: Sovereignty in the Age of Globalization* 1995

Robert Pollack, *The Faith of Biology & the Biology of Faith:
Order, Meaning, and Free Will in Modern Medical Science* 2000

Ira Katznelson, *Desolation and Enlightenment:
Political Knowledge After the Holocaust, Totalitarianism, and Total War* 2003

Lisa Anderson, *Pursuing Truth, Exercising Power:
Social Science and Public Policy in the Twenty-first Century* 2003

Partha Chatterjee, *The Politics of the Governed:
Reflections on Popular Politics in Most of the World* 2004

David Rosand, *The Invention of Painting in America* 2004

George Rupp, *Globalization Challenged:
Conviction, Conflict, Community* 2007

Lesley A. Sharp, *Bodies, Commodities, and Technologies* 2007

Robert Hanning, *Serious Play:
Desire and Authority in the Poetry of Ovid, Chaucer, and Ariosto* 2010

Douglas A. Chalmers, *Reforming Democracies:
Six Facts About Politics That Demand a New Agenda* 2013

Philip Kitcher, *Deaths in Venice: The Cases of Gustav von Aschenbach* 2013

ROBERT L. BELKNAP

PLOTS

WITH AN INTRODUCTION BY
ROBIN FEUER MILLER

COLUMBIA UNIVERSITY PRESS
NEW YORK

Columbia University Press
Publishers Since 1893
New York   Chichester, West Sussex
cup.columbia.edu

Library of Congress Cataloging-in-Publication Data

Names: Belknap, Robert L. author.
Title: Plots / Robert L. Belknap ; with an introduction by Robin
Feuer Miller.
Description: New York : Columbia University Press, 2016. | Series:
Leonard Hastings Schoff memorial lectures | Includes bibliographical
references and index.
Identifiers: LCCN 2015039972 | ISBN 9780231177825 (cloth : acid-free
paper) | ISBN 9780231541473 (e-book)
Subjects: LCSH: Plots (Drama, novel, etc.) | Fiction—Technique.
Classification: LCC PN3378 .B44 2016 | DDC 808.3—dc23
LC record available at http://lccn.loc.gov/2015039972

∞

Columbia University Press books are printed on permanent
and durable acid-free paper.
Printed in the United States of America
c 10 9 8 7 6 5 4 3 2 1

COVER DESIGN: CHANG JAE LEE

TO CYNTHIA

CONTENTS

PREFACE

This book grows out of the 2011 Leonard Hastings Schoff Memorial Lectures at the Columbia University Seminars. In deference to the spirit of interactive intellection those seminars have fostered since the 1940s, I have tried to keep some of the lectures' oral quality and do without formal notes. The bibliography does include all the works I cite and a number of others that may interest the curious, but it does not pretend to cover the field. When I know of an English translation of one of the works that I cite, I list it in the bibliography even when I used the original and provided my own translation. When many editions or translations exist, I give chapter, scene, or other standard indicators in the text, as such information may be more helpful, though sometimes less precise, than a page number.

I am particularly grateful to the Woodrow Wilson Fellowship Program, the Bellagio Center, the Kennan Institute at the Smithsonian Institute, the John Simon Guggenheim Foundation, the National Endowment for the Humanities, and the International Research and Exchanges Board (IREX) for providing me with time and resources, sometimes explicitly for this book and sometimes for other undertakings that left their mark on it.

These lectures gestated over many years, while I studied or taught at Princeton, the University of Paris, and Columbia, Leningrad, and Hokkaido Universities, using their libraries and the Bibliothèque Nationale, the Library of Congress, the Lenin (now National) Library in Moscow, several libraries and archives of the Russian Academy of Sciences, and the New York Public Library in those days when its rich and accessible collections made it a world center for Slavic studies. This book carries a deep intellectual debt to all those institutions, as well as to the teachers, colleagues, and students whose words and ideas inform the text.

In somewhat different form, parts of several chapters have appeared in the *Slavic Review*, the *Slavic and East European Journal*, *Dostoevsky Studies*, *Dostoevskii: Materialy i issledovaniia*, and a *Festschrift* for Malcolm Jones published by Cambridge University Press. These articles and a number of conference papers have provoked responses from colleagues which corrected errors, added readings, and made this book a genuinely collective enterprise. Three educational inventions at Columbia—the undergraduate Core Curriculum, the graduate-level Harriman Institute, and the University Seminars for scholars and specialists—added a breadth of disputatious learning to the professional intercourse in the Slavic Department. Finally, Deborah Martinsen read an early version and improved it immensely, while Nancy Workman has edited the final draft, caught errors, clarified confusions, and made it into a proper manuscript. Although I am deeply grateful to many, many colleagues, I claim full personal credit for all the errors and inadequacies in the text.

INTRODUCTION

ROBIN FEUER MILLER

The greatest part of a writer's time is spent in reading, in order to write:
a man will turn over half a library to make one book.
—James Boswell, *The Life of Samuel Johnson*

A legendary scholar and teacher, both in Columbia University's Department of Slavic Languages and Literatures and in its trademark Core Curriculum, Robert L. Belknap (1929–2014) also served as acting dean of Columbia College, director of the Harriman (then Russian) Institute, and director of the University Seminars. His written work ranges from intensely focused books and essays on single works by single authors to a treatise, *Tradition and Innovation: General Education and the Reintegration of the University*, coauthored with Richard Kuhns, which embraced in the broadest terms the institution and goals of the university and of education. In the last decades of his life, Belknap was at work on his magnum opus—his book on plot. Having heard his lectures on various aspects of his work, I, like many others, began to imagine a voluminous tome in the making, almost a textbook or an encyclopedia of plots—a work unlike Belknap's other idiosyncratic, creative, and forcefully argued writings, more oriented toward collecting and synthesizing past theories and knowledge.

Collect and synthesize the volume certainly does, but like Aristotle's *Poetics*, this book is short, fiercely and economically argued, and, above all, persuasive, punctuated with the kinds of "aha" moments that

Belknap had described in other contexts. He even presents his reader with a kind of meta "aha" moment when he defines two kinds of recognition that readers may experience: "If the audience knows what one or more characters do not, the audience experiences the powerful effect of dramatic irony. If the audience does not know, it experiences its own 'aha,' rather than a vicarious one" (56). In *Plots,* he has brought his focus to bear not only on particular works, but also on the broad question of plot—plot as it plays out in monumental, profoundly complex works. Always intrigued by theory, diagram, design, and structure, Belknap was also a critic of these enterprises when they failed to elucidate, became artificial, or simply functioned as ends in and of themselves. He always retained his capacity to see and to acknowledge if the emperor was wearing no clothes. How typical of Belknap to produce a magnum opus that is particular, profound, original, and short.

Beach-walkers who collect shards of beautifully polished sea-glass, molded and smoothed by sea and sand, its transparency rendered into translucence, find it increasingly difficult to come upon such treasures, probably because plastic bottles now substitute for glass and float on the sea in indestructible hordes or wash up onto the sand as non-degradable trash. *Plots* is a rare sea-glass, emerging from the ocean ready to be picked up by any walker who likes to traverse that boundary between sea and land, between the ocean of literature and experience and the drier sands of discourse about them. The sea-glass is a result of them both.

Belknap's *Plots* is both pragmatic and philosophical. It abounds with trenchant definitions and bold epigrams while probing and appreciating paradox and mystery. Belknap asks the kind of questions most of us avoid because they are simultaneously too difficult and too basic to answer: What is an incident? Can an incident be as large as a whole novel or as small as three sentences? What is a summary? Are plots fractal? Most tautly argued literary theories find short or minor works to serve as elucidating examples. Belknap cheerfully tackles *King Lear* and *Crime and Punishment* to test his propositions.

Plots is as pithy as its title. In it, Belknap distills a lifetime of abundant reading and creative thinking about what plots are and how they work. Consider whether the following three paragraphs are a summary of Belknap's book or a map of what is to come:

Literary plots deserve still more study. Plots arrange literary experience. Plot summaries need more serious study. The fabula arranges the events in the world the characters inhabit; the siuzhet arranges events in the world the reader encounters in the text. Authors can relate one incident to another only chronologically, spatially, causally, associatively, or narratively. Plots are fractal, formed from incidents that are formed from small, similarly shaped incidents. The best authorities consider plots and incidents to be tripartite, with a situation, a need, and an action. But siuzhets and the incidents that form them have two parts: an expectation and its fulfillment or frustration.

The plot of *King Lear* operates purposefully but also reflects the creative process. For integrity of impact, stages, actors, and the audience need a unity of action. Shakespeare replaced the Greek unity of action with a new thematic unity based on parallelism. Shakespeare uses conflict, the righting of wrongs, the healing of an inruption or disruption, and other standard plotting devices, but his recognition scenes move us most. Shakespeare prepares for his recognition scenes with elaborate lies. In *King Lear*, Shakespeare used elaborated lies to psychologize the Gloucester subplot. Tolstoy and Tate preferred the comforting plots of *Lear's* sources to Shakespeare's, but Shakespeare had considered that variant and rejected it.

The plot of *Crime and Punishment* draws rhetorical and moral power from the nature of novel plots and from the European and Russian tradition Dostoevsky inherited and developed. European novelists elaborated or assembled incidents into plots long before critics recognized the sophistication of the new genre in plotting such subgenres as the letter novel and the detective novel. Dostoevsky shaped and was shaped by the Russian version of the nineteenth-century novel. In reinventing the psychological plot, Dostoevsky challenged the current literary leaders. The siuzhet of part I of *Crime and Punishment* programs the reader to read the rest and to participate actively in a vicious murder. The one-sidedness of desire and violence in *Crime and Punishment* is more peculiar to Dostoevsky's plotting than *Dostoevshchina*. Critics often attack *Crime and Punishment* for a rhetoric that exploits causality in ways they misunderstand. The epilogue of *Crime and Punishment* crystallizes its ideological plot. The plots of novels teach novelistic, not poetic, justice.

Belknap would sometimes paraphrase, in all seriousness, Samuel Johnson's irreverent witticism about an unread book: "I've not read it, sir, but I have held it in my hand." Belknap agreed with Johnson that holding a book in one's hand is in fact a significant prelude to actually reading it. Readers who have already held *Plots* in their hands, perhaps admiring its neat, handy, and compact size, may have also glanced at its table of contents and noticed its eighteenth-century-like chapter headings. They will recognize the three paragraphs above as those titles converted into narrative.

When rendered as a set of paragraphs rather than chapter headings, these sentences become a summary of Belknap's overall argument rather than the mapping of chapters for a reader moving through the text in time. They are also, Luther-style, the propositions that Belknap nails to the critical wall, propositions simply and boldly stated at the outset, defended with seriousness, logic, and learned irreverence in each of the chapters. Any one of these sentences or headings could serve as the operating thesis for a much longer study; yet Belknap achieves, even with his self-imposed constraint of brevity, a completeness for each argument. Are we willing to accept that plots are fractal? Have we ever thought that the incidents forming the siuzhet of a narrative might have only two parts, instead of the customary three? Do lies really fuel the plots of so many of William Shakespeare's tragedies? Are desire and violence truly one-sided in Fyodor Dostoevsky's novels and more essential than suffering for his plots? What is novelistic justice as compared to poetic justice? How can such a small book formulate and pose so many questions, let alone dare attempt to demonstrate solutions to them?

Belknap does not shy away from unfashionable words like "great" or "monumental." Neither will I. (By reveling in such words and using them appropriately, he reminds readers of their value, of their moral and aesthetic weight.) Belknap was one of the finest and most original writers on Dostoevsky in the twentieth century. Bucking the trend of lengthy books about lengthy novels, his two books on *The Brothers Karamazov*, both small and concise like this one, remain essential reading for inquisitive readers of that great Russian author. For generations of *Karamazov* readers, Belknap has somehow merged with the novel, becoming a shadowy but intermittently observable figure, almost like the eponymous Kugelmass in Woody Allen's early story, "The Kugelmass Episode," whom readers discover lurking in *Madame Bovary*. Many of Belknap's students and readers find him lurking in the corners of Dostoevsky's works, shaping our reading.

Belknap's distinctive style reflects his intellect; his predilection for reducing complex incidents to their elemental units not to simplify so much as to expose their intricacy; and his talent for marshaling evidence from numerous sources, high and low, in his task of persuasion. He also casually uses words that send readers to the dictionary and reward us for the effort—for example, "inruption" (already cited in the table of contents of this book), "achrony," or "proairetic," all useful words that make one wonder at the rarity of their general usage. Likewise, among the many other works of fiction, drama, philosophy, history, and criticism to which he will allude lightly but meaningfully are some about which the reader may well have been completely ignorant. Take, for example, his passing allusion to Mary Cowden Clarke's *The Girlhood of Shakespeare's Heroines: A Series of Fifteen Tales*: although cited in the context of a discussion about motivation in Shakespeare, it may inspire the reader to think in different ways about Dostoevsky's heroines as well. For example, what did little Dunya and Raskolnikov fight about as children? How did little Sonya react when her mother died? "In fiction," Belknap tells us, "an unknown or assertedly nonexistent cause is not just unknown but simply not there" (100). Though we may choose to ponder such hypothetical questions, we cannot answer them. They are simply outside the causal system of the work at hand. Earlier, Belknap had argued that "fiction obviates much of the philosophical debate about causation" (22). In a novel or play, on the contrary, causation is "by fiat" (24).

Among those readers who are also teachers of literature, how many of you, like me, hasten in your introductory lectures to get definitions and discussions of plot out of the way at the outset so as to focus on more interesting and seemingly complex questions about such matters as character, motivation, space, narration, discourse, metaphor, and detail? Perhaps you teach your students about the differences between the fabula and the siuzhet, making passing reference to the Russian formalists or to René Wellek and Austin Warren's *Theory of Literature*. Your students may memorize the definitions of these two moderately useful terms and quickly come to substitute in their minds the narration for the siuzhet, or some similar formulation. Then it is on to other matters. The notion of fabula gets even shorter shrift. As merely the incidents or events of the story in the chronological order in which they actually occur, the fabula may seem to operate as a simple background that allows the author to create the intricate narrative fabric of what is generally assumed to be the far more interesting siuzhet.

Within a few pages of reading Belknap's work, however, one begins to be persuaded that in fiction the plot—in its various manifestations of summary, of fabula, of siuzhet, of the relation of incident to incident, or of parallel plot to parallel plot—is the heart of the matter. Belknap defines the fabula as "the relationship among the incidents in the world the characters inhabit" and the siuzhet as "the relationship among the same incidents in the world of the text, a one-dimensional array of words encountered one after another in the time system of the reader" (16–17). A plot suggests a path that can lead to the understanding of a particular work that is more telling and even more significant than the ending of a work (a place where one routinely looks for meaning). Plot is most certainly not an element to be whisked to the periphery. Moreover, the fabula, "where causation plays a crucial structural role" (17), is at least as complex and slippery to define as the siuzhet. Throughout, Belknap demonstrates how the fabula is frequently pitted against the siuzhet because it is multidimensional in space and time, whereas the siuzhet is not.

Belknap's book will undoubtedly be read in conjunction with other general works on plot and narration, especially the now classic *Reading for the Plot: Design and Intention in Narrative* by Peter Brooks. At the outset, Brooks writes:

> This is a book about plots and plotting, about how stories come to be ordered in significant form, and also about our desire and need for such orderings. Plot as I conceive it is the design and intention of narrative, what shapes a story and gives it a certain direction or intent of meaning. . . . Plot is so basic to our experi-

ence of reading, and indeed to our very articulation of experience in general, that criticism has often passed over it in silence as too obvious to bear discussion. Yet the obvious can often be the most interesting, as well as the most difficult, to talk about.

(Brooks, xi)

Belknap, albeit undoubtedly in agreement with much of what Brooks has suggested, builds up to a discussion of plot from its most discrete elements, incidents. He emphasizes its most fundamental definition: "Plots are ways of relating incidents to one another. . . . Plots are purposeful arrangements of experience" (3, 4). Moreover, he sees a special urgency in coming to terms with a fuller understanding of plot as we have known it up through the present day because of the "huge array" of new questions emerging from ubiquitous new technologies that offer interactive possibilities of plot which have yet to be explored.

Few theorists have addressed the question of plot summary with the sustained scrutiny that Belknap brings to bear upon it. From the outset and throughout the book, Belknap contends that "plot summaries deserve serious theoretical attention" (7). "Like a translation," he maintains, "a plot summary tries to represent a text. . . . Indeed, some argue that the summary of a book *is* the plot of the book, with all the burden of significance and power that implies; others argue that the only proper summary of *War and Peace* is the book itself, that summary is impossible." Summary, in his view, aspires to the same accuracy as translation but is equally subject to the imprint of the summarizer's or translator's tastes and idiosyncrasies: "Like translators and other writers, summarizers may fail to see or understand the thing they are presenting, may intentionally or unconsciously impute their own ideas or obsessions to their subjects, or may construct straw enemies to attack as a way of satisfying their social cultural, psychological, or other needs." At this point the reader-critic may squirm or smile, for of course all of us, Belknap included, are to some extent both summarizers and translators. At various moments throughout, Belknap wittily illustrates his own sharp insight about the paradox—both the distortions and the potential illuminations—plot summaries can offer by presenting summaries either by others (most notably Tolstoy's of *King Lear*) or his own.

While Tolstoy's dislike of Shakespeare, especially *King Lear*, is well-known, Belknap exposes the tactics Tolstoy uses, unfairly, to express his dislike (and perhaps hide his jealousy). "Unlike *CliffsNotes*," as Belknap points out, the kind of summary Tolstoy employs in *King Lear* presupposes the reader's acquaintance with the text and is thus "a text about a text" (72). Belknap argues that Tolstoy particularly hated the plot of the play, and by analyzing Tolstoy's summary of it, he exposes the precise nature of Tolstoy's detestation. He observes, for example, that Tolstoy's summary of the tragic moment when Lear brings Cordelia's body on stage is actually eight words longer than the passage it is summarizes. Tolstoy writes: "Lear enters with the dead Cordelia in his arms, notwithstanding the fact that he is past eighty and sick. And Lear's horrible delirium begins again, which makes one ashamed, like an unsuccessful joke. Lear demands that everybody howl, and sometimes thinks Cordelia is dead, sometimes that she is alive. 'Had I,' he says, 'your tongues and eyes I would use them so that the heavens would crack'" (Tolstoy, *PSS*, 35:235, quoted at 71). I leave it to readers to savor the trenchant analysis that follows as well as the general insights about plot in both *King Lear* and its sources.

Of course, Belknap himself frequently proposes his own summaries, which are no less idiosyncratic and instructive than Tolstoy's. His summary of *King Lear* includes the following: "The symmetries are constructed to confront the audience with two old sinners whose wicked children play on their overwhelming credulity to gain their property and then destroy them, despite the self-sacrificing efforts of their faithful, loving children" (64). As this example demonstrates, Belknap's persistent habit of carefully reducing things to elemental units frequently results in a deeper understanding of a complex set of interrelated incidents, i.e., a plot. Later, when analyzing the plots of *The Arabian Nights* and *Don Quixote* and how they are recycled to some degree in Dostoevsky's fiction, he concludes with another summary: "The grinding paradox of *Crime and Punishment*—that we care about the well-being of a calculating, self-absorbed hatchet-murderer—rests in part on the picaresque way the narration obsessively focuses our attention on him as he rushes from crisis to crisis" (83–84). Moreover, he demonstrates how the readers of the novel become "accessories after the fact" (106) following the murder, so that we slip into the same algorithmic alternations as Raskolnikov.

Belknap often deploys humor to clarify and sharpen his argument. The reader thus encounters a series of cheeky moments along the way. In discussing, for example, the diverse meanings that the terms *fabula* and *siuzhet* have acquired during the decades of critical scrutiny of them, he writes, "For the purposes of this study, the best translation for *fabula* is 'plot' and the best translation for *siuzhet* is also 'plot'" (16). Then follows a sober explanation of why this is so. I am reminded of the moment in Gogol's *Dead Souls* when the inveterate liar Nozdryev drags his exhausted guest Chichikov to the boundary marker at the edge of his huge estate only to tell him that everything on this side of the marker is "mine," and everything on the other side of it is "mine" too. By defining both *fabula* and *siuzhet* as "plot," Belknap demonstrates the interdependence between these two terms and emphasizes that the most important aspect of plot is perhaps the relationship among incidents. As he observes, the fabula and the siuzhet in fact often strain against each other: "The reader can come to know the fabula only through the siuzhet, and the author cannot imagine a siuzhet without some fabula to express; an account has to be of something" (17). What Belknap labels as the "literariness" of any work comes from the interplay between the two. Likewise Nozdryev, the liar and gambler, perhaps owns nothing on either side of that marker.

Before embarking on the insightful readings of *King Lear* and *Crime and Punishment* which form the second and third parts of this book, Belknap offers up a humorous but illuminating consideration of "a small work of art." It is indeed small; Belknap cites it in its entirety. It comes from Rabelais's *Gargantua*: "The appearance of St. Gertrude to a nun of Poissy, in labor" (39). I won't give away his reading of this "work" in terms of its fabula and siuzhet, but readers will discover in it the ideal prelude to the extended analysis of the two monumental literary works which follows.

Belknap hypothesizes that Shakespeare "sacrificed the causal tightness that had served classic drama so well in order to build thematic tightness around parallel plots" (50). He scrutinizes the varieties of lies and lying operative in *King Lear*, the lines of causality they create, and the kinds of recognition scenes they engender both in the characters and the audience. He suggests that in Shakespeare's plays, "except in a single play, . . . virtually every recognition scene is generated primarily out of a lie, not an error" (59). He explores the reasons that Shakespeare may have preferred lies to errors as an instrument for complicating and generating plots. Moreover, he notes that "each lie is a little drama, with at least the rudiments of a plot" (61). Many readers may find themselves ready to accept Belknap's surprising, speculative claim "that Shakespeare, having created the central canon for the English sonnet and the central canon for English comedy and tragedy—history plays having been in place before him—was preparing himself to invent the modern English novel when he was cut off by death" (58).

Belknap's propensity for humor does not obviate his capacity for high solemnity. As he prepares for his excursion through *Crime and Punishment*, he writes, "A great book is a fearsome thing, and always tempts a reader to talk about something else" (80). Although his profession demands "that I seek order in the text," he knows that "texts, like the world, aren't orderly—they're messy." It has been customary among many scholars who have written about the evolution of Dostoevsky's narrative style and his plots to rather quickly dispense with what has been considered the outmoded eighteenth-century epistolary form that Dostoevsky used for his first short novel, *Poor Folk* (1846). Belknap, however, discovers in this early epistolary work both the bedrock for Dostoevsky's subsequent plots as well as for his own argument, extending through the great writer's entire oeuvre, that Dostoevsky did not, contrary to a persistent popular notion, glorify suffering as an ennobling way-station on the path to virtue and salvation.

Before laying out his reading of *Crime and Punishment*, Belknap also anchors Dostoevsky in the Russian tradition that preceded him, ranging from Karamzin through Pushkin, Lermontov, Gogol ("The plot of all of Gogol's greatest works is very simple: 'Paradise Lost'" [96].), and Chernyshevsky, although "Dostoevsky challenged them all by psychologizing their causal systems"—their plots (100). He cites what he labels Henry James's "cardinal rule" for narrators—that they be consistent: "James's narrators may be wise or foolish, even insane or fanatic, but must be consistently whatever they are, so that 'the interest created, and the expression of that interest, are things kept, as to kind, genuine and true to themselves'"(92). Belknap compellingly demonstrates how, in marked contrast, a hallmark of Russian narration is the constant violation of this rule in myriad ways, thus linking the development of the

Russian novel to the eighteenth-century European tradition of "more flexible narrators" that was increasingly rejected by European novelists of the nineteenth century but embraced by the Russians. Belknap's reading of Gogol's "The Tale of How Ivan Ivanovich Quarreled with Ivan Nikiforovich" humorously, movingly, and incisively illustrates these points, and I urge readers to give special attention to it.

Belknap offers several readings of the plot of *Crime and Punishment*, each of which leads to different outcomes. In one of these, part I of the novel becomes a novel called *Crime*, and the remaining parts are *Punishment*; in another, Dostoevsky's epilogue is its own work of art to which the novel proper is but a "massive prologue." "This prologue loads the names, the events, and even certain words with meaning that enables Dostoevsky to address his readers with great economy of exposition after hundreds of pages spent training them" (127). Needless to say, each of these plot-focused readings is convincing. Surprisingly, Belknap turns back to the little-read work of Ernest Simmons to find a counterpoint to many of his arguments—especially for his reading of the epilogue—rather than to some of the more recent critics of Dostoevsky. I expect that Belknap was perhaps being diplomatic in his choice of "straw men," although his fellow critics might well have welcomed a more frontal engagement. Belknap's extended reading of the controversial epilogue to the novel, which Konstantin Mochulsky has vividly described as a "pious lie," becomes an occasion for his important ruminations about confession and repentance. Raskolnikov repents in the epilogue after an intricate series of largely incomplete confessions throughout the novel proper. "Confession is not the result of repentance. Rather, it is the means to it" (125). It is has been frequently noted that Raskolnikov rehearses his crime, but Belknap delineates how he also rehearses his confession and his repentance.

Perhaps what is most exciting about Belknap's *Plots* is that it rewards the reader with a plot of its own. How many works of criticism have a plot? At the outset of his study, Belknap declares that the distinction between fabula and siuzhet, while a standard part of the critical vocabulary, has most often been regarded as "an interesting peripheral concern" (18). By the end of this book, he will likely have persuaded many readers that this very distinction often "leads to the most useful ways of understanding large works of literature." By choosing *King Lear* and

Crime and Punishment as his "case studies" and subjecting them to probing, close readings that examine chains of causalities, parallel plots, and depictions of how the reader, in a plot of her own, must unceasingly negotiate among all these plots, Belknap has marshalled irresistible evidence to argue that plot—more than character, setting, detail, or conclusion—is the sine qua non.

In his final chapter, Belknap permits himself a last big question: "After many pages discussing what plots are, how they work, and what they can accomplish, it is time to address a final question, what plots mean, and the attendant hermeneutic question, how that meaning is knowable" (129). Belknap unpacks the question of meaning by discussing examples of both low culture (James Cameron's film *Titanic*) and high culture (*Anna Karenina*). In both cases he asks the question of "whether or in what cases we can use the ending of a work of literature to learn the meaning of the work" (132). Suffice it to say, Belknap answers this question (I will not be a spoiler here) through an exposition and analysis of genre and plot. As Belknap concludes his book with a stunning discussion of how novelistic justice is different from poetic justice, the reader may begin to think of actual, personal, human experience in terms of the endless, creative tension between fabula and siuzhet. It is a current but vague cliché that one forms and embraces "one's own narrative." Belknap indirectly but powerfully offers us a jagged, vital example of what that might mean—where fabula and siuzhet are as operative in real life as in fiction, and where different kinds of time, space, lies, truths, memories, desires, and recognitions collide and coalesce into something experienced simultaneously by each individual as both a narrative and a plot.

WORKS CITED

Allen, Woody. "The Kugelmass Episode," in *Side Effects*, 59–79. New York: Random House, 1981.

Brooks, Peter. *Reading for the Plot: Design and Intention in Narrative.* New York: Random House, 1984.

Wellek, René, and Austin Warren. *Theory of Literature*. New York: Harcourt Brace, 1949.

PLOTS

PART I

LITERARY PLOTS DESERVE STILL MORE STUDY

I

Plots Arrange Literary Experience

This book explores some of the ways creative and critical minds have dealt with literary plots. Plots are ways of relating incidents to one another, and critics as diverse as Vladimir Propp, Georges Polti, Sigmund Freud, and Aristotle have insisted on how few of these ways really work. I will start with a set of first principles at least as reductionist as any of theirs and then plod into the combinatorial morass where theories confront actual creation, fall, gall themselves, and, if they are very lucky, gash gold-vermillion.

Back when it was fashionable to do so, I once saw a play in which actors drew their lines from a hat before declaiming them. I've spent better evenings. Works that make a single point seldom entrance me even when I like the point, but this time the point was wrong too. The play set out to show the value of the aleatory, the randomness art needed if it was to imitate the universe, but it really showed through negative example that the arrangement of the action was more important than diction, spectacle, thought, music, or even character, all of which might, at least in part, survive a good shuffling. At that time, as in Aristotle's time, each of these other elements had its advocates. Eric Bentley was asserting the importance of stage business, one of the modern equivalents of spectacle. The Irish playwrights asserted and exploited the glories of dialect, eloquence, and the other aspects of diction. The late Stalinists were sacrificing all else to correctness of thought; Eugene O'Neill was making similar sacrifices to the compellingness of his characters. Alan Lerner pronounced that, at least in musical comedy, plot was quite immaterial.

Since then, the swing of fashion has brought plot back into repute in scholarly and creative circles. Some authors make effective plots instinctively, while others have never learned, although many splendid critical minds have been describing the features common to successful literary plots for millennia, and many less impressive minds have been turning those descriptions into prescriptions.

When I started to read about literary plots, I promptly found myself in a forest of multilingual terminology where one can wander indefinitely, lost in the tangles, or entranced with the byways. I realized that the English word "plot" translates the Russian words *tema, plan, fabula,* and *siuzhet,* each of which in turn is a transliteration of a Greek, Latin, French, or other word and has several other meanings in each respective language. In English, the components of a plot are called "anecdotes," "motifs," "themes," "incidents," "episodes," "moves," "plots," "subplots," "thememes," "functions," "motifemes," etc. In this book, I shall try to keep my terminology clear while confronting the same problems that have made others so inventive in the past.

Plots are purposeful arrangements of experience. In political plots, part of the experience is man-made; other parts—the rising of the moon, for example—are not, but plotters still organize relationships between them. In literary plots, even the rising of the moon is man-made, though it must either mimic moonrises that are not man-made or else introduce oddness into the plot, as the behavior of the sun does for different purposes in the biblical Book of Joshua, Plautus's *Amphitryon,* and Lewis Carroll's "The Walrus and the Carpenter." Both literary and political plots have purposes their authors enunciate, purposes their authors conceal, and purposes embedded in the author's nature or past too deeply for deliberate control. The language, imagery, rules, structures, and conscious and unconscious purposes of political plots deserve continuing study, but this book will only treat literary plots. Plots deserve study at this moment because over the centuries many of the finest literary minds have raised questions about them that should be answered as completely as possible before a huge array of new questions emerges in response to the interactive possibilities that are beginning to reside in computers, with innumerable alternatives available at the click of a mouse or the touch of a keyboard button, and with vast new complexities in the relation between the audience and the author.

2

Plot Summaries Need More Serious Study

In Aristotle's *Poetics*, the Greek word *mythos* has two separate meanings, both of which survive in the English word "plot" today. It can mean the organization of the incidents in a literary work (1450a) or the story that can be summarized, whether the original or one drawn from Homer or some other source (1451b). This book will concentrate on the first meaning, but this chapter is about the second.

The theoretical and critical attention that translation studies, reception studies, source studies, and the use of quotation, allusion, literary influence, and other forms of intertextuality have received contrasts startlingly with the broad inattention paid to literary summaries. Summaries are not rare. Most secondhand bookstores are flooded with *Reader's Digest* condensed novels, several to the volume; students buy thousands of copies of *CliffsNotes* and *Monarch Notes* and incur the wrath of their teachers for handing in millions of papers and exams that are nothing but plot summary. The inattention cannot be ascribed to historical unimportance; for a millennium, the West knew Homer primarily through summaries, and much of ancient epic and drama is still entirely lost except for summaries. Tzvetan Todorov once claimed to have based his Boccaccio studies on summaries and not the original *Decam-*

eron, and migratory plots may well move more often through summaries than through translations.

Plot summaries deserve serious theoretical attention. Philosophers and authors have often claimed that literature represents or imitates something—a moral action, a human life, a revolution, a particular psychological state or experience, etc. But many of these represented things are hard to describe with much precision. Like a translation, a plot summary tries to represent a text, a set of black marks on a page that are more "there" for a literary scholar than many objects of representation. Indeed, some argue that the summary of a book *is* the plot of the book, with all the burden of significance and power that implies; others argue that the only proper summary of Leo Tolstoy's *War and Peace* is the book itself, that summary is impossible.

Like a translation, a summary aspires to accuracy, though subject to a number of constraints, some present in all texts, some peculiar to this genre. Like translators and other writers, summarizers may fail to see or understand the thing they are presenting, may intentionally or unconsciously impute their own ideas or obsessions to their subjects, or may construct straw enemies to attack as a way of satisfying their social, cultural, psychological, or other needs. It has often been argued that all art is an abstraction of reality, that a painting abstracts the third dimension, that a drawing abstracts color and perhaps shading too, and that the abstract art of this century abstracts many other features of recognizability. Literary summaries are not only abstract art, but are also the art of abstraction. In summaries, the universal literary need to select and omit emerges in a peculiarly vivid and examinable form.

The aspiration to accuracy raises many further theoretical questions. At one extreme, the nihilists deny that there is any meaning resident in the original text beyond what the summarizers and other members of the critical community impute to it. At the other extreme, the computer experts claim that a machine can summarize a collection of texts rather more usefully than the people usually available for the task. Some machines simply copy out the first and last paragraph or the first and last sentence of every other paragraph of the text. A more intricate machine counts the uses of different words in the text and matches that count with the word count for the universe of texts in a particular field. Singling out the list of words more prevalent in this text than in the field, it selects the paragraphs in which these words occur most and prints out these paragraphs.

These synecdochic approaches, using parts to summarize the whole, work better with the scientific articles they were designed for than with the plots of novels and plays, where they might be more useful for thematic analysis. Only the wondrous unselfconsciousness of certain natural scientists, however, would consider such machines objective, since different definitions of the lexicographic universe, different lengths of prevalent word lists, and different ways of arranging the paragraphs could produce substantially different summaries that reflect the identities of different programmers.

Charles and Mary Lamb used an even less objective approach to write their *Tales from Shakespeare* for very young girls, hoping "that no worse effect will result than to make them wish themselves a little older, that they may be allowed to read the Plays at full length." Their technique was partly synecdochic, using quoted lines when they could, but also using their own words to bridge gaps and make William Shakespeare's text clearer and more accessible to young readers. In the final speech of *Measure for Measure*, for example, Duke Vincentio of Vienna says, "Dear Isabel, / I have a motion much imports your good; / whereto, if you'll a willing ear incline / what's mine is yours, and what's yours is mine" (5.1.548-51). In his introduction to the play, George Lyman Kittredge comments on this marriage proposal: "We may infer that Isabella gives up her purpose of becoming a votary of Saint Clare, . . . but this is not stated, and the play leaves the audience guessing,—as was doubtless Shakespeare's intent."

The Lambs summarize Shakespeare's four lines as follows:

The Duke offered himself again to the acceptance of Isabel, whose virtuous and noble conduct had won her prince's heart. Isabel, not having taken the veil, was free to marry: and the friendly offices, while hid under the disguise of a humble friar, which the noble duke had done for her, made her with grateful joy accept the honor he offered her; and when she became duchess of Vienna, the excellent example of the virtuous Isabel worked such a complete reformation among the young ladies of that city, that from that time none ever fell into the transgression of Juliet, the repentant wife of the reformed Claudio. And the mercy-loving duke long reigned with his beloved Isabel, the happiest of husbands and of princes. (*Tales from Shakespeare*, 218–19)

This passage offers an exaggerated example of several characteristics I have noticed about many summaries. It is much longer than the original, it removes the ambiguities, and it adapts the passage to the needs or expectations of its readership, giving the tale a happy ending like those in the fairy tales young girls already knew.

In adapting *Measure for Measure* "for very young children," the Lambs display their pre-Victorian frankness in discussing the law "dooming any man to the punishment who should live with a woman that was not his wife" (202). One has only to compare Gilbert and Sullivan's *Mikado*, where the crime in a comparable plot was flirting, or the post-Victorian American edition of the Lambs' tales, where *Measure for Measure* is omitted altogether. Yet the Lambs do omit the raunchy subplot of *Measure for Measure* involving the fortunes of Lucio, Mistress Overdone the bawd, and her group of prostitutes, a subplot where syphilis plays the role that AIDS plays in some theatrical explorations of debauchery today. Curiously, Alexander Pushkin imitates this silence of the Lambs when he adopts *Measure for Measure* as a source for "Angelo." Pushkin has been accused of many things, but not, as far as I know, of Victorian prudery. The classicist in him may well have led him to omit this subplot and achieve unity of action by concentrating all his attention on the title role at the expense of the associative richness that gathers about the themes of inevitable death, uncontrollable desire, and the exploitation of women. I would, however, suggest a simpler explanation: perhaps Pushkin drew his "Angelo" not just from Shakespeare's play, but also from the Lambs' summary.

Because of external evidence, I have taken literally the Lambs' protestations that their tales were merely an introduction to the full text; but in other cases, the stated purpose may protest too much, much like the disclaimer in formal type at the beginning of every volume of *CliffsNotes*: "These notes are not a substitute for the text itself or for the classroom discussion of the text, and students who attempt to use them in this way are denying themselves the very education that they are presumably giving their most vital years to achieve." This disclaimer reminds one of the surgeon general's warnings on cigarette packages. This mimesis of the enforced warning suggests a complicated reading of it. At the outermost level, it states a truth to which most of us subscribe: even if the plot summary details the plot of a play (and Aristotle is correct when he calls the plot the central element in the play), the plot summary alone can only replace the play for the most primitive of purposes. At the second level, both the publisher and the readers of *CliffsNotes* know that thousands of students use *CliffsNotes* as a substitute for the text and that the disclaimer establishes a kind of naughty solidarity between the publisher of this substitute and the student misusing it. At the third level, *CliffsNotes* are far better than nothing, and its patronizing pose is educating those adolescents whose rebelliousness and sense of intellectual inadequacy would incapacitate them for reading texts sanctioned by the cultural and educational establishment. In this way, the format and introduction reduces high culture to low culture, even when *CliffsNotes* present the full text, as they do for several Shakespeare plays. Here is canon-making in reverse. Shakespeare had written for royalty and groundlings and had been pirated as only low culture tends to be, especially before the appearance of the First Folio in 1619. From then on, generations had made him a figure of awe—"What needs my Shakespeare for his honored bones the labors of an age in piled stones" (John Milton) or "Others abide our question. Thou art free" (Matthew Arnold)—until *CliffsNotes* demystifies him and attracts to him the kind of person who would become a smoker *because* the surgeon general called it dangerous or become a drinker in the 1920s *because* Prohibition laws forbade it.

Like the Lambs' tales, *CliffsNotes* sometimes carry the spirit of the original work beyond what the author enunciated. The account of Tristram Shandy's accidental circumcision in chapter 18 of book 5 is a case in point:

> "—'Twas nothing.—I did not lose two drops of blood by it—'twas not worth calling in a surgeon, had he lived next door to us — thousands suffer by choice what I did by accident." "The chambermaid forgot to put a ******* ***• [chamber pot] under the bed." Susannah raises little Tristram up to the window seat, lifts the

window with one hand, and asks the child if he will, for this once, "**** *** ** *** ******." Down came the window "like lightening upon us;—Nothing is left,—cried Susannah—nothing is left for me but to flee the country."   (Parish, 67)

This summary presents the original synecdochically with considerable skill, but the commentary on the next page is every bit as Sternian as the original text:

The story of the accidental circumcision—not an accident of the same magnitude as the other accidents—is sprung on us first by Tristram's saying that the consequences of something were trivial and then by showing us the scene itself. The use of asterisks for the indelicate object (the chamber pot) and the indelicate action is itself delicate and interesting: the reader easily succeeds in filling in the words—one letter for each asterisk, with a space between words—and he is pleased with his detective work; then, if he is a Victorian reader, he is offended at the author's coarseness.
                                                                 (Parish, 68)

In *CliffsNotes*, Sterne's text is reduced to a little more than a page each of summary and commentary per chapter. The commentary simply adds to the commentaries of Tristram, Susannah, Uncle Toby, Walter Shandy, Yorick, etc., upon the fall of a window sash. Like Sterne's text, it is punctuated with dashes, and like that text, it implies the imbecility of the reader. The Notes make the delicate and interesting distinction between the phrase "chamber pot" and the phrase "piss out of the window," spelling out the first and leaving the second in asterisks. *Tristram Shandy* is about consciousness, particularly the reader's, and this passage, like much of Cliff's booklet, is really a poor man's Sterne, the experience of self-consciousness for a hypo-student who has to have everything explained.

But there are cases with no disclaimer where the summarizer quite openly expresses the hope of making further reading unnecessary. Russian book reviews in the nineteenth century, and more recently, often have this purpose. In Soviet times, a standard format emerged for summarizing materials the censor would have had to cut had they appeared in other formats. Many books began with the phrase "Western critics are falsifying the history of Russian literature," continued with accurate and clear summaries of several Western books to which their readers had little or no access, and concluded, "Our scholarship must combat these lies." This transparent frame for the summaries deceived no one, least of all the censors, but it made the literary obeisance that permitted publication. In nineteenth-century Russia, the literary criticism in one thick journal would contain long summaries of books and materials in other thick journals. Summaries are one of the things that made them, in translation, "fat." Let us examine Nikolai Chernyshevsky's summary of Alexander Ostrovsky's *Poverty's No Crime*, a comedy that was often restaged by the theatrically savvy producers of the nineteenth century. Like the Lambs, Chernyshevsky mingled his summary with other material, but unlike them, he felt no obligation to clarify the playwright's meanings. He concludes his summary of act I as follows:

> We have recounted the first scene in such detail that readers, doubtless exhausted even by an abridged report of all these irrelevancies and inconsistencies, incoherent with the real content of the play, exhausted with all these confidants, prologues, monologues which contain not a shadow of the dramatic, will ask us to abbreviate our telling of the two remaining scenes.

Chernyshevsky's desire to spare his reader an encounter with the full text was as sincere as the Lambs' desire to woo a young reader toward the full text of their beloved Shakespeare, and for the symmetrical reason, as he expresses it in the first paragraph of his article: "Mr. Ostrovsky's new comedy is unbelievably weak (*slaba do neveroiatnosti*)." This desire to spare the reader the trouble of reading a text need not, however, be motivated by a distaste for the text. In the 1994 holiday issue of Continental Airlines's *Sky Mall: The World's In-Flight Shopping Mall*, for example, IntelliQuest, which describes itself as "The Knowledge Company," advertises its summaries with the highest praise for the books summarized:

ACQUIRE AND APPLY THE WEALTH AND KNOWLEDGE
CONTAINED IN THE WORLD'S
100 GREATEST BOOKS
WITHOUT A LIFETIME OF STUDY.

Never before has so much knowledge and wisdom been brought together into one comprehensive collection!

Like most intelligent people, you've always wanted to read the great books of world literature, to learn about their authors and acquire their timeless knowledge, wisdom and insights. But, like most people, because your time is so limited, you'll probably never have the time. Now you can, thanks to *The World's 100 Greatest Books Audiocassette Collection*—and you can do it in only a matter of weeks!

LISTEN TO EACH BOOK IN ONLY 45 MINUTES

Based on a powerful new learning system that allows you to quickly learn and incorporate a large body of knowledge into your daily life and conversation, this comprehensive package consists of two volumes of 50 cassette tapes, with one book on each 45-minute side.

Despite their condensed presentation, the mood and richness of the original works have been preserved to a remarkable degree. And by reinforcing the audio presentation with printed Knowledge Maps, you can absorb the lessons of great literature in the most efficient manner possible.

For those who long to incorporate a large body of knowledge into their daily life, this advertisement might be misleading, but for those who hope to incorporate the *appearance* of a large body of knowledge into their conversation, it might offer just what they need. As Cole Porter put it much earlier, "The girls today in society / Go for classical poetry" (395).

In one sense, however, we are always dealing with plot summaries when we deal with plotted literature. A novel or even a play is far too big to keep in our rapid-access memory. We can memorize and recite it, but even as we recite it, the parts we are not currently reciting retreat into longer-term storage places, so that the only way any of us can work with the whole plot of a play is to make our own summary and work with that. Intellectuals use their own summaries rather than those from *CliffNotes* or *IntelliQuest* in order to foreground the elements that are of particular use for their purposes. In argumentation, this selectiveness may blind us to evidence against us, but when we are using a text as the basis for a literary work, the elements of plot that migrate from culture to culture, language to language, genre to genre, or merely from one work to another reflect the needs of the author who reuses them, whether artistic, psychological, political, religious, or for other reasons.

As an instrument of literary polemic, summary, like translation or parody, bears a special relation to its subject matter, since the subject matter is verbal, and the polemicist, like the translator, has temporary control of his reader's access to the original text. Such summary removes the unessential from a text and leaves the identity, the meaning, or the form intact. For a given text, therefore, as many different summaries are possible as there are views of what is essential; more, in fact, because summaries can add elements to the text.

Modern plot studies began with plot summaries, or with the ways plots or parts of plots move from text to text. Classicists were discussing the ways Plautus and Terence adapted the Greek New Comedy of Menander and others even before most of the Menander texts had been retrieved. Terms like *contaminatio* were used for the merger of two inherited plots. An anthropologist like J. G. Frazer would devote a dozen volumes to the variants of a single plot that Lord Macaulay had summarized two generations earlier in eleven words: "the priest who slew the slayer and shall himself be slain." Others have argued that there are only seven basic plots. In 1895 Georges Polti listed thirty-six dramatic situations. His introduction linked that fact to a corollary, that there are thirty-six emotions. His epigraph invokes the names of Johann Wolfgang von Goethe and Friedrich Schiller as authors who had tried, but unlike Polti, failed to find the thirty-six plot situations that had been posited, but not enumerated, by Carlo Gozzi. The folklorists Antti Aarne and Stith Thompson compiled multivolume dictionaries of parallel plots, ranging from Iceland to Micronesia, sometimes migratory and sometimes parallel creations.

These huge lifeworks of scholarship are an endless delight for any curious mind. They offer the shock of recognition, the encounter with a familiar plot in an unfamiliar context, plus a rich array of lore that no reader could have encountered seriously in its entirety. So, with no disrespect for the sometimes noble art of the summarizer, the remaining chapters of this study will tend to ignore the aspect of a plot that can be summarized and focus instead on Aristotle's other definition of a plot, plot as the relationship among the incidents.

This focus follows many of the structuralists who compared Polti, Aarne, and such organizers of data to lexicographers, and innocently accepted Samuel Johnson's definition of a lexicographer as "a harmless drudge." These structuralists have asserted the superiority of grammarians, morphologists, and other kinds of linguists, who sometimes revel in complexity, or, at their best, reduce complexities to wonderful simplicities.

3

The Fabula Arranges the Events in the World the Characters Inhabit; the Siuzhet Arranges the Events in the World the Reader Encounters in the Text

Like many philosophical definitions, Aristotle's definition of a plot as the relationship among the incidents leaves us with two words to explore instead of the one we started with. What is a "relationship," and what is an "incident"? This chapter and the next will discuss the first of these questions. Let us begin with a relatively simple question: where do such relationships exist?

To answer this question, I need to offer my own definitions for two favorite terms of the Russian Formalist critics in the 1920s, *fabula* and *siuzhet*. Unlike the French Structuralists, who contributed invaluable terminological precision to the Slavic discoveries of an earlier generation, the Formalists lacked the time and probably the analytical inclination to worry very much about terminology. Boris Tomashevsky, the fiercest of these Leningrad scholars, warns us that in criticism "the terms *fabula* and *siuzhet* are used with the most diverse meanings, sometimes the direct opposite of the way I use them here" (134). For the purposes of this study, the best translation for *fabula* is "plot" and the best translation for *siuzhet* is also "plot." In both cases, the plot can be defined as the relationship among the incidents, but these two sets of relationships exist in two different worlds. The fabula is *the relationship among the incidents in the world the characters inhabit,* a multidimensional, intricately interconnected array where events may happen simultaneously in different places, where causation plays a crucial structural role, and where sequences of events exist in the time system of the characters' lives. The siuzhet is *the relationship among the same incidents in the world of the text,* a one-dimensional array of words encountered one after another in the time system of the reader.

To some, this pair of terms comes close to the classical terms of rhetoric, *inventio* and *dispositio,* the first designating the discovery of the raw literary material, often in literary or other sources, and the second the way the author organizes that material in the new text. This terminology presumes that authors start with content and then impose form upon it. Rhetoricians have made this assumption in many periods of history, but it fell out of fashion about a century ago as literary thinkers became conscious that formal decisions like "I need a surprise ending" often preceded the selection of particular content to put at the end. The more sophisticated view, as expressed by Benedetto Croce and others, is that form is inseparable from content. This view works well for most literature, but we have already discussed how the material for translations and summaries does have a separate anterior existence.

Other scholars have linked the fabula with Ferdinand de Saussure's "signified" and the siuzhet with his "signifier," or associated the two with the deep and surface structures Noam Chomsky describes in his *Cartesian Linguistics* and elsewhere. These pairs of words from discourse about signs and sentences share one paradox with the fabula–siuzhet pair: in all three, each element is logically prior to the other, depending upon one's point of view. The reader can come to know the fabula only through the siuzhet, and the author cannot imagine a siuzhet without some fabula to express; an account has to be of something. In small forms, like fairy tales, these two kinds of plot tend to track one another rather closely, but in larger forms, like epics or novels, they often diverge. In the siuzhet of the *Odyssey,* for example, Odysseus's meeting with Nausicaa precedes his meeting with Polyphemus the Cyclops. In the fabula, Odysseus meets Polyphemus long before he meets Nausicaa.

The fabula, and each incident within it, has a primarily mimetic structure; it imitates the ordering of events in the life that nonfictional people live. The siuzhet, and each of its parts, has a manipulative or rhetorical structure, shaped to make the reader share and even participate in the action of the text. It may mimic the literary genres of nonfiction, as in a novel in letters, but the one-dimensionality of the text determines its central organization. In most novels and epics, most incidents exist in both the fabula and the siuzhet, but the fabula may occasionally contain unrecounted incidents that are arguably not a part of the siuzhet, while the siuzhet will almost always contain similes, digressions, and other elements whose incidents have nothing to do with the world in which the characters act and are acted upon. When Milton calls book 9 of *Paradise Lost* "not less but more heroic than the wrath / Of stern Achilles on his foe pursu'd / Thrice fugitive about Troy Wall" (9.14-16), the flight of Hector plays no part in the lives of Adam or Lucifer, and thus is not a part of the fabula, but it briefly interrupts the account of those lives in the siuzhet. Tomashevsky distinguishes between works of literature where the fabula is central and those where the siuzhet matters far more, but in practice much of the literariness of virtually any substantial work of literature comes from the interplay between the two. Dramatic irony, for example, occurs when the siuzhet outpaces the fabula and characters living within the fabula act in ignorance of some fact in their world that the audience already knows. In the classical detective story, on the other hand, the fabula outpaces the siuzhet and leaves the reader in ignorance of who done it, which at least one of the characters knows full well. Such matters will enter my later discussion of *King Lear* and of the detective story known as *Crime and Punishment*.

This distinction between fabula and siuzhet has been a standard part of the critical vocabulary for the better part of a century, most often as an interesting peripheral concern. For this book, it leads to the most useful ways of understanding large works of literature.

4

Authors Can Relate One Incident to Another Only Chronologically, Spatially, Causally, Associatively, or Narratively

Within the fabula or the siuzhet, two incidents can be related in very few ways. One can occur before or after another, near or far from it, because of it, resemble it, or be narrated within it. In the fabula these relationships differ from those in the siuzhet. Let us start by looking at time in the siuzhet.

Chronologically, incidents in the siuzhet can come before or after other incidents, in the text and in the reader's or audience's experience of the text. An incident in the siuzhet may also interrupt another incident that therefore brackets it. These are the only chronological relationships possible in the siuzhet, though sometimes, as in *The Arabian Nights* or *Tristram Shandy*, interruptions can effloresce magnificently. In general, all these chronological relationships exploit the fact that the siuzhet, like time itself, is one-dimensional. Gotthold Lessing's *Laocoön* calls attention to many of the implications of this fact. Novels with pages that can be shuffled may confuse the issue slightly, as was intended. Scholars in Mikhail Bakhtin's tradition link time and space into a multidimensional chronotope that I have subdivided for expository clarity and will explore further.

In the fabula, the Before–After relationship is more complicated. Its zero degree, simultaneity, can be as important as the absence of an ending on a word in an inflected language. In the world the characters inhabit, incidents may occur simultaneously as well as happen before or after other incidents, or bracket or interrupt them. In practice, this possibility constitutes a key difference between the fabula and the siuzhet. In addition, within the fabula the Before–After system may even be eliminated entirely. A catalogue of incidents, or a bill of particulars, may involve incidents in the lives of the characters which exist in no particular chronology. If fiction were history, one could argue that the timing had simply been lost, but in a literary fabula, pure achrony is possible in a list of incidents whereas, except in the shuffled novel, incidents in the siuzhet always come before or after one another.

Spatially, in the siuzhet the world can occasionally be two- or three-dimensional, especially in drama, where incidents can occur at different places on the stage; or in a Sergei Eisenstein film, where each frame aspires to two-dimensional design; or in Kabuki theater, where each moment tries to relate the interacting characters, props, and scenery into a visual tableau, as early ballet did in the West. In calligraphy and in certain printed Baroque poetry, the incidents presented on a page can also assume a visual relationship, but the normal shape of the siuzhet in verbal texts is one-dimensional, beautifully adapted to the shape of time but not of space, which causes problems in the way the siuzhet presents the fabula.

Spatial relationships between incidents occasionally play a crucial part in the fabula. When they do, the relationship will often be associative as well. Asians sometimes talk about six directions: North–South, East–West, and Up–Down. In the Western tradition, we tend to pair these directions and talk about three dimensions, but Down–Up would doubtless be the briefest summary of the *Divine Comedy*, and the key relationships between Dante's incidents tend to be spatial along this axis, much as Southness is central to the spatial organization of Edgar Allan Poe's *Narrative of Arthur Gordon Pym*. The television series *Upstairs-Downstairs*, on the other hand, uses the directional signs more for association with social class than as directions, much as Southness is used in many American Civil War stories to denote a culture as well as a spatial quality. In the Sherlock Holmes stories, it has been observed that incidents are related by insideness, with its connotation of coziness, and outsideness, with its connotation of adventure in the fearsome London jungle. Incidents may be linked or separated by the way they are located, affecting the causal system, as in Evgeny Shvarts's play *The Treasure*, where characters talk across a gulf that can be crossed only by making a four-day detour. Such a location permits verbal causation but excludes physical causation. In a Buster Keaton movie, characters can hunt each other on a ship for minutes on end, each always on the opposite side or on the wrong deck for finding the other.

In the siuzhet, we have seen that the chronological system usually cannot be distinguished from the spatial, which normally has to be reduced to a single dimension. In the fabula, Bakhtinians think of the two systems as a single chronotope, much as how in their equations physicists think of time as a fourth dimension. In the fabula of some science fiction and fantasy writing, such as Lewis Carroll's *Sylvie and Bruno* or his Alice books, independent or interacting time-space systems may coexist. Alice does not meet the White Knight before or after the events in her real world, but in a separate looking-glass time system, and the rabbit hole leaves her not under land but in wonderland. One time-space system is enough for most books, however. When Lessing, Samuel Taylor Coleridge, and many others discuss the problem of representing this multidimensional world in the one-dimensional world of a literary text, they find it as basic in literature as the problem in the visual arts previously mentioned: abstracting a three-dimensional world to a two-dimensional surface through the various systems of perspective, or representing motion in rock or bronze.

Bakhtin's studies of the history of the chronotope shape part of my discussion of Fyodor Dostoevsky's novelistic plotting. Here, it is sufficient to indicate that the chronological and spacial relationships pit the fabula against the siuzhet, because the fabula, which is multidimensional in space and time, is accessible only through the basically one-dimensional siuzhet. The simplest way to shift simultaneity to the chronological system of the siuzhet is to say, "Meanwhile, back at the ranch," and carry the reader sequentially through a spatial shift. Authors have a rich body of techniques for solving this Laocoön problem, but over the centuries it has become not so much a problem as a great resource for producing literary effects. Much of the artistry critics have studied for millennia rests on the exploitation of the difference between time and space in the fabula and time and space in the siuzhet. Homer was praised in classical times for beginning in medias res, telling the middle of the fabula at the beginning of the siuzhet. This body of techniques includes the whole world of interruption, delaying mechanisms, suspense, foreshadowing, sideshadowing (to use Gary Saul Morson's term), and *curiosité*, that cousin of suspense which puzzles readers as to what is going on at the present moment rather than what will happen next, which is the domain of suspense. These mechanisms take different forms at different periods and in different genres, and will enter this study in various restricted contexts.

The *cause/effect* relationship is central for the fabula and is sometimes, but not always, important for the siuzhet, where it takes the form described by Viktor Shklovsky and the other Formalists as the *motivirovka*. The *motivirovka* must not be confused with the characters' motivations for action in the fabula. The best translation of *motivirovka* may be "rationale." The rationale justifies the existence of a text or some part of it: a manuscript found in a bottle or a story told for a particular purpose. The play within a play in *The Taming of the Shrew* takes its rationale from the introductory play, which many modern productions omit entirely. In a *skaz*, a story with a socially defined narrator, the rationale for the story may be an incident, like the shipboard meeting between the framing narrator and the horsebreaker in Nikolai Leskov's *Enchanted Wanderer*; or it may be an implied situation, as in a Damon Runyon story presented in the language of a Broadway tout with no framing introduction. When one incident becomes the rationale for another, as when Scheherazade's encounter with the Caliph explains the existence of her stories, the reader experiences in the siuzhet the equivalent of causal linkage between two incidents in the fabula. But very often in the siuzhet, cause and effect play a minor role.

Even in the fabula, where cause and effect are central, incidents are occasionally unrelated causally: "And then another adventure befell me"; "By a strange coincidence," and so on. Fiction obviates much of the philosophical debate about causation. David Hume may argue that we deduce causal relationships from consistent sequences of events, but while narrators in a novel or a play may rely on such deductions—"I threw the hammer at him and he died"—they also have the power to declare events causally related or unrelated, sometimes in ways designed to puzzle the reader. Such perverse or unexplained causation by pure fiat plays a large part in the mystery of certain lyrics, such as John Webster's:

> Call for the robin redbreast and the wren,
> Since o'er the shady groves they hover
> And with leaves and flowers do cover
> The friendless bodies of unburied men.

(The White Devil, 5.4.96–99)

Or John Keats's:

> And that is why I sojourn here
> Alone and palely loitering,
> Though the sedge is withered from the lake,
> And no birds sing.

("La Belle Dame Sans Merci")

In these passages the causal words—"since," "why," and "though"—set off rationalizing reverberations in the reader's mind that open up worlds of enchantment and alternative reality. Such cases of expressed causality with restricted justification are as rare as their opposite, suppressed or distorted causation, as in the case of the character in the first scene of Nikolai Gogol's *Inspector General*, who claims that his colleague has smelled of alcohol ever since his mother dropped him as a baby, denying the causal tie with the man's current lifestyle that the audience is expected to realize. Such causation or non-causation by pure fiat at first leads us out of the world of everyday life, but then, since there is no such thing as a pure literary experience unmediated by the rest of our experience, literary or other, our rationalizing instincts collide with our literary experience. The knowledge of genre, of literary allusion, of social background, of our own psychology all shape our responses to a work of literature, but the most basic plot relationships interact with some of the most basic patterns of our mind. When the interaction is dissonant, our reactions are the standard regressions to childhood, a giggle, or that creepy feeling that is also produced by the uncanny. Most commonly, however, causation by fiat works in parallel with causation perceived by the reader. In etiological tales, like many of those we know from Rudyard Kipling or Claude Lévi-Strauss, an incident may cause not an incident but a situation we already accept, such as an existing anatomical peculiarity or culinary custom. In other words, the integrity of the work comes in part from the fact that the causes the narrator cites make sense of some aspect of the reader's extra-literary experience.

Most of the time, the cause and effect system in the fabula works in close parallel with the chronological system, but one whole area of causality can be relatively independent of the Before–After relationship. Psychological causation, which we call "motivation," may look to the future as easily as to the past. When a subsequent incident motivates a prior one, we call it the prior incident's "goal." When a prior incident motivates a subsequent one, we call the subsequent one a "response." Motivation constitutes the most intricate and subtle part of the causal way of relating one event to another. When I turn to the theory of drama, we will encounter Aristotle's view that every event in a drama has to be causally related to every other, and when I turn to the theory of the novel, we will encounter E. M. Forster's sense that the causal system powers the plot.

Incidents can be *embedded* in other incidents in dramatic, lyrical, and other genres, as well as in genres that we consider primarily narrative, like epics and novels. The rationale or *motivirovka* for an incident is often provided by embedding it in another incident. When Othello talked of

the most disastrous chances,
Of moving accidents by flood and field;
Of hairbreadth scapes i' th' imminent deadly breach;
Of being taken by the insolent foe
And sold to slavery; of my redemption thence
And portance in my travel's history ...

(*Othello*, 1.3.135–40)

Desdemona loved him for the dangers he had narrated, and he loved her that she did pity them. Here, in the siuzhet, Othello's questioners provide the *motivirovka* for the presence of these adventures in the play, while in the fabula, the narration of these adventures provides the motivation for Desdemona's love. In this way, the causal system of the siuzhet works closely with the system of embedded materials in the fabula and the siuzhet.

When characters recount their own actions or those of others, the act of narrating stands between the audience and the narrated action. The anonymous narrator of many novels is just as much a created character as the prologue or any character in a drama, and characters in many literary genres tell stories of one sort or another. Embedding can establish a narrative hierarchy among incidents. A character in one incident narrates an incident in which a character narrates a third incident. In *The Arabian Nights*, such subordination can go down to the fifth level, interworking with the other kinds of relationships. By merely existing at the narrated level, each story prolongs Scheherazade's life at the narrating level, but often stories are introduced because they are similar to something that has happened at a higher narrative level or because they caused it, and sometimes they happen before, after, or during incidents at other levels, or in the same place.

This use of embedded incidents lies near the artistic center of *The Arabian Nights*—and that is rare in literature—but *The Decameron*, *The Canterbury Tales*, *Don Quixote*, *Tristram Shandy*, and a host of other works illustrate the importance of this kind of relationship in the evolution of the novel, a matter I will discuss when I try to locate the plot of *Crime and Punishment* in the history of novelistic plots. For now, it will suffice to repeat that incidents related by being embedded complicate the relation between the fabula and the siuzhet. Othello does not woo Desdemona on stage; his wooing enters the fabula of the play through two conflicting accounts whose interaction influences the Venetian duke in the causal system of the play. Through this narration, his narrated adventures also become part of the fabula and their narration causes Desdemona to react to them. One character's fabula can be another's siuzhet when incidents are embedded in narrated incidents.

In both the fabula and the siuzhet, incidents can also be related *associatively*. Such relationships can take many forms, sometimes by the fiat of a narrator or a character and sometimes through the reader's direct apprehension. An incident may be identical to another, or similar, or (in theory, at least) bear no resemblance. Both identical and totally unrelated incidents are rare. Two incidents with zero points in common would probably be impossible in history or in the science of pattern recognition, but fiction permits the pure case by fiat, where a reliable narrator says that two incidents have no resemblance at all, although I cannot think of an example. At the other end of the spectrum, exact repetitions can occur on any scale. The most perfect example of large-scale repetition occurs not in fiction but in fictional fiction: Pierre Menard's *Don Quixote* surpasses the *French Don Quixote* and other imitations by being closer to Cervantes's, in fact by being identical with it. Even such repetition cannot fully duplicate the original, as Jorge Luis Borges's narrator points out in "Pierre Menard, Author of the *Quixote*," because the existence of Cervantes's text makes this new one different.

On a smaller scale, similarity can be regarded as the repetition of certain elements in a whole. Repeated passages can serve many purposes. In epic, when the whole Achaean expedition is in danger, Agamemnon's offer to reward Achilles's service is elaborated twice in virtually the same words. But even though the identity of the repeated passage is changed somewhat by the existence of the first passage, the length of the repetition has attracted considerable critical attention. In lyric, however, repetitions of a refrain or a line commonly occupy a larger percentage of the total poem, growing in meaning as the context changes, as in Thomas Nashe's refrain which, as the next chapters will show, is in itself a fabular incident: "I am sick, I must die. Lord have mercy on us." On a scale smaller than a single line, repetitions tend to fall under the Aristotelian heading of diction, including many of the standard rhetorical devices: anaphora; the whole world of versification, with the repetition of consonantal sounds in alliterative poetry, of vowel sounds in assonant poetry, of both in rhymed poetry, of quantitative patterns in Roman poetry, of pitch patterns in Greek poetry, of loudness patterns in English poetry; and in general, as Roman Jakobson points out, the manipulation of whatever feature carries the most phonemic meaning in a given language—an observation that helps explain why English experiments in quantitative poetry or Russian experiments in syllabic poetry never established vigorous movements. In his "Grammatical Parallelism and its Russian Facet," Jakobson quotes Gerard Manley Hopkins when he observes: "The artificial part of poetry, perhaps we shall be right to say of all artifice, reduces itself to the principle of parallelism. The structure of poetry is that of continuous parallelism, ranging from the technical so-called parallelism of Hebrew poetry and the antiphons of Church music to the intricacy of Greek or Italian or English verse" (399).

In the world of prose plots, parallelism plays almost as important a role as Hopkins gives it in the world of diction, but in most cases the parallel takes a form more like rhyme or metaphor than perfect repetition. That is, some elements of an incident recur and some are changed. Whole genres of literature center on such partial parallelism, and at the smallest level, most literature contains metaphors that sometimes compare things but often compare actions, a corner of plot studies that Christine Brooke-Rose has amply explored.

At the grandest level, the three- and fourfold allegorical systems of late classical, medieval, and more recent literature, or typological readings of the Bible, are based on such parallels. Allegorical plays and novels do exist, but the traditions that are central in this book use less elaborated parallels. A traditional allegory is a mapping of one plot onto another, with each element in one corresponding to an element in the other and each relationship among elements in one corresponding to a relationship among elements in the other. To achieve such correspondences, the author of one plot must be attuned to the author of the other, who in most cases is assumed to be God. The possibility of fourfold allegory implies that we are living in an orderly universe, where history has the same relationships among its parts as a human being's salvation has, or the entire creation and salvation of the universe has, or a text written by an inspired author has, because the Creator has left his signature on every element in His creation. Plato claims that justice in a republic was the same virtue as justice in a human being, and that the parts of a human soul match those in a state and stand in the same just or unjust relationships to one another. A monomaniac runs his life as a tyrannical state runs itself.

When critics impose allegory upon works of literature not written with allegory in mind, the results can sometimes be ingenious, sometimes noble, sometimes laughable, and sometimes sick. Allegorization can also save a precious text. The Song of Solomon was too sensuous for certain ascetics in the Christian church, but survived in the canon as an allegory of the relationship between the Church and God. But

King Lear and *Crime and Punishment* have not responded well to allegorical treatment. Elizabethan drama and nineteenth-century novels use parallelism instead of allegory to lead their audience to generalize thematically.

Pattern-recognition theorists often claim that everything resembles everything else. Computers in the post office that read addresses must be programmed to know which squiggles matter and which do not. Large works of literature do just that to readers. They have the time to train us to feel and sometimes see the points of similarity and contrast that matter, whether we are dealing with the two plots of *King Lear* and other Shakespearean plays or with what Jan Meijer called "situation rhyme" in Dostoevsky's novels. But these are discussions for the chapters of practical criticism that will come after these theoretical chapters.

5

Plots Are Fractal, Formed from Incidents That Are Formed from Smaller, Similarly Shaped Incidents

I have defined a plot as the relationship among the incidents in a work of literature and devoted two chapters to characterizing the five kinds of relationships and the two worlds in which they can exist. This chapter will discuss an even more basic question: what, if anything, is an incident?

One can argue, of course, that an incident is any part of a text that a reader decides to call an incident. In this extreme position, all characterizations of incident in principle are equally valid and in practice seek their justification not in any epistemic dependence on the text but in the elegance, coherence, ideological usefulness, psychological gratification, or richness in resonance of the remarks the text stimulates the reader to make. Roland Barthes seems at first to be making this argument in *S/Z*, but stops short of complete arbitrariness:

> The proairetic sequence is never more than the result of the artifice of reading; whoever reads the text amasses certain data under some generic title for actions (stroll, murder, rendezvous), and this title embodies the sequence; the sequence exists when

and because it can be given a name, it unfolds as the process of naming takes place, as a title is sought or confirmed.   (19)

In this passage, Barthes assumes that the text will talk back: a sequence needs a name if it is to be perceived, or even to exist, but to be confirmed, a name needs something at least arguably present and concrete, a sequence in the text. Barthes's restrained epistemic nihilism lacks the philosophical impregnability of the extreme position. The word "confirmed" deprives him of the privilege of ignoring the text, but it also avoids the question we tend to ask when Freudians, Marxists, postmodernists, or sophomores tell us portentously that the human mind can never react with complete objectivity to any matter under consideration: so what else is new?

Barthes's chief vulnerability lies not in the question of how the reader projects his categories upon the text but in the study of migratory plots that exists in many different pieces of folklore or other objects of explication. In the critical traditions where modern plot studies began, it takes strong devotion to theory to treat as an artifact of reading an incident that has retained its identity through many different texts, often for millennia. The devoted nihilist could always answer, "The identity of the migratory plot is in itself an artifact of the reader's perception," preserving ideological consistency at the expense of a body of experience to which Aarne, Thompson, and Jean Girandoux, who wrote the play *Amphitryon 38,* have devoted enormous attention. An ingenious nihilist could challenge the exact boundaries of any incident since incidents change, taking on the coloration of the culture or the genre where they appear, but the generations of philologists who have explored such changes could attack the nihilists' adversarial consistency by claiming that if incidents could talk, they might say, "I change; therefore I am." This appeal to experience is no more sophisticated than Samuel Johnson's kicking of a rock to prove the world was there, but this book rests modestly on just such a rock.

The Russian Formalist critics of the 1920s were trained in Saussurian structural linguistics and inherited Alexander Veselovsky's positivistic dream of a clear and unambiguous science of literature that would account for everything by using simple terms and consistent rules. Tomashevsky, Propp, and Shklovsky all begin discussions of plot with a deferential acceptance of Veselovsky's definition of a plot (siuzhet) as "a complex of motifs" and a deferential rejection of his characterization of a motif. Veselovsky drew from the folklorists the perception of a motif as a persistent entity, like the killing of a dragon or the abduction of a princess, that could move from work to work across the barriers of time, space, language, class, and culture, even penetrating communities which could not understand the original meaning of a particular motif. In the tradition of Max Mueller, he explains that a motif is a

> formula which in early society answered questions which nature everywhere posed to man or which reinforced those especially vivid impressions of reality which seemed important or were recurrent. The mark of a motif is its figural single-termed schematicism; such are the irreducible elements of primitive mythology and folktale: someone steals the sun (an eclipse); a bird bears lightning-fire from the sky....
>
> The simplest type of motif can be expressed by the formula $a + b$: the wicked hag dislikes the beauty—and assigns her a life-threatening task. Each part of the formula is subject to transformations; b especially undergoes expansion; the tasks may be two, three (the favorite folk number), or more.... Thus a motif would grow into a plot.
>
> (*Istoricheskaia poetika*, 494–95)

In this passage, Veselovsky is establishing the bases for an ambitious effort to adapt rules already developed for folk plots to more extensive and intricate narrations, a task that would later attract investigators as different as Shklovsky and Claude Bremond. Within the two pages which I have abridged here, Veselovsky shifts from the atomic perception of motifs as the many irreducible units out of which a plot may be assembled to the alchemical perception of a motif as a single unit, which may grow into a plot through repetition and whose forms and uses are restricted by culturally inherited rules. None of the Formalists objected to this double way of looking at a motif or to the coexistence in Veselovsky's text of two different ways of perceiving and presenting the world, but most of their work leaned more toward the structural than the algorithmic.

Tomashevsky saw no conflict between the two approaches when he called a plot (*tema*) "a certain more or less integral system of events, one ensuing from another, one linked with the other," and goes on to describe these events as follows:

> Before organizing a plot, it must be divided into parts, then be hung on the narrational core. The concept of plot is a *summarizing* concept, uniting the verbal material of a work. A whole work may have its plot, and at the same time each part of a work possesses its own plot. Such a separation out from a work of parts each unified by a particular unity of plot is called the analysis of the work....
>
> Through such analysis of a work into units of plot, we finally arrive at *irreducible* parts, at the most minute fragments of plot material: "Night fell," "Raskolnikov killed the old woman," ... etc. The plot of an irreducible part of a work is called a *motif*. Basically, every sentence possesses its own motif.
>
> (*Teoriia literatury*, 136–37)

In this strongly positivistic passage, Tomashevsky writes like a mathematician describing sets whose members are sets whose members are sets. He would not have known about fractals, which only became popular with mathematicians in the past few decades. A fractal curve has kinks, and kinks on the kinks, and smaller kinks on those kinks, and so on indefinitely, so that fractal patterns repeat themselves on a smaller and smaller scale and an enlargement of any part of a fractal curve will look exactly like an unenlarged portion of the same curve.

Tomashevsky asserts that plots can be analyzed into units that are also plots, so that no generic difference distinguishes "Raskolnikov killed the old woman" from "Night fell," although one summarizes a hundred pages of text and the other recapitulates two words of text. He understands that the irreducible plotlet and the scheme for a whole novel are merely the extreme ends of a spectrum of plot sizes.

Propp carries Tomashevsky's attack on Veselovsky to its logical conclusion:

> The motifs which [Veselovsky] cites as examples do decompose. If a motif is something logically whole, then each sentence of a

tale gives a motif. (A father has three sons: a motif; a stepdaughter leaves home: a motif; Ivan fights with a dragon: a motif; and so on.). . . . But let us take the motif "a dragon kidnaps the tsar's daughter." . . . This motif decomposes into four elements, each of which, in its own right, can vary. The dragon can be replaced by Koshchej, a whirlwind, a falcon, or a sorcerer. Abduction can be replaced by vampirism or various other acts by which disappearance is effected [*sic*] in tales. . . . The final divisible unit, as such, does not represent a logical whole.

(Morphology of the Folktale, 12–13)

Propp's apparent quarrel with Veselovsky centers upon the word "irreducible," which Veselovsky himself did not intend to preclude internal structure, as his formula "$a + b$" indicates. But Propp really was objecting to the vast and messy collection of variables Veselovsky, like a lexicographer, would have to deal with, unlike Propp, a morphologist who pursued a limited and ordered collection of variables. Propp finds that Veselovsky's motifs relate to particular plots but cannot be generalized. To ascertain the rules for a folklore plot, Propp must isolate himself from particular folktales and deal with "functions" that can be reduced not to sentences like "Raskolnikov killed the old woman," but to abstractions like "interdiction, interrogation, flight," whose very bloodlessness makes them applicable to many tales. He defines a function as "an act of a character, defined from the point of view of its significance for the course of the action" (21), and adds that the functions of characters serve as stable, constant elements in a tale, independent of how and by whom they are fulfilled. They constitute the fundamental components of a tale, and the number of functions known to the fairy tale is limited.

6

The Best Authorities Consider Plots and Incidents to Be Tripartite, with a Situation, a Need, and an Action

Propp's functions are certainly fundamental, but they may not be incidents. Fractals, being mathematical forms, can replicate the same patterns from the infinitely large down to the level of the infinitesimal, but incidents, according to many thinkers in Athens, Leningrad, Paris, and elsewhere, are more like water. Unless we know the scale of a map, we cannot always know whether it represents a gulf, a bay, or a tiny inlet, but in all of these—and even when we descend to the level of buckets, drops, and molecules—we are still talking about water. But when we divide a molecule of water, we are no longer dealing with water because we have lost the basic internal structure of H_2O. In the same way, an incident may be so small that it cannot be reduced to a combination or an expansion of other incidents, but even this smallest incident has an internal structure of elements that, taken separately, are not incidents any more than hydrogen and oxygen separately are water. The critical community today would usually say that "Night fell" lacks the internal structure that would warrant the name "incident" and that Propp's functions may need to be taken not as incidents but as parts of a larger unit that follows a fixed formula. Propp himself expressed this very idea:

Morphologically, a tale (*skazka*) may be termed any development proceeding from villainy[,] . . . a lack . . . through intermediary functions to marriage[,] . . . or to other functions employed as a denouement. . . .

This type of development is termed by us a *move* (*khod*). Each new act of villainy, each new lack creates a new move. One tale may have several moves, and when analyzing a text, one must first of all determine the number of moves of which it consists. One move may directly follow another, but they may also interweave; a development which has begun pauses, and a new move is inserted. Singling out a move is not always an easy matter, but it is always possible with complete exactitude.

(*Morphology of the Folktale*, 92)

Bremond argues that if this basic pattern for a "move" is indeed fixed, if Propp's labors have proved that functions can only take fixed positions in a fixed pattern (which Bremond doubts), then the real base unit, the narrative atom, is not the function but the series. Like Propp, Tomashevsky distinguishes three kinds of very basic units, but for him the most important seems to be what Propp passes over as intermediary in the passage just quoted. For Tomashevsky, "motifs are easily distinguished according to their importance. Dynamic motifs take the first position, then preparatory motifs, and then motifs defining the situation, etc." These three kinds of motif correspond—in reverse order—with Algirdas Julien Greimas's three types of narration: "*les énoncés descriptifs, les énoncés modaux, et les énoncés translatifs.*" The French Structuralists took many of their ideas from the Russian Formalists, but laid them out with greater elegance than any of the Russians except perhaps Shklovsky. Greimas, an Eastern European operating in France, defines the first kind of motif as something that can be expressed in a sentence with the verb "to be" and an adjectival word or phrase; the second can be expressed with a modal verb such as "wants to," "ought to," "needs to," etc.; and the third with an active verb. The hero is in a special state; he needs something; he achieves it. This sequence seems to define linguistically what the Russian Formalists were struggling to convey but never found the terminology to explain succinctly.

Shklovsky expresses this internal structure for a plot more clearly than anyone before the French Structuralist clarification of Formalist concepts:

> I have already said that if we take some typical story-anecdote, we will see that it represents something complete [*zakonchennoe*]. To take for example as one's material: a shrewd answer which gets the person out of a tight spot, we have the explanation of the tight spot into which the character has fallen, his answer, and a particular resolution; such is the structure of "trickster novels" in general. For example, the man who is marked after a crime by having a lock of hair cut off cuts it off from all his friends and thus saves himself; similarly in a story of the same type about a house marked with chalk (*1001 Nights*, Andersen). Here we see a definite . . . cycle which sometimes unfolds with descriptions, characterizations, but which in itself represents something resolved. Several such stories can form a more complicated structure, being set into a single frame, so to speak, united into a single plot cluster. (*Theory of Prose*, 68)

To sum up this traditional definition of an incident: it may be as large as a whole novel or as small as three sentences, it may be treated from the creator's point of view as one of the building blocks for a text or as the generating entity whose transformation forms the text, it may be treated from the reader's point of view as one of many components discovered by analysis or as the simple outcome of a summary, but the tripartite internal structure of an incident emerges near the center of the best investigations of this question, as it did when Aristotle characterized the plot of a good drama as something with a beginning, a middle, and an end. A beginning is something which demands no prior material, like the exposition of a situation using the verb "to be." An end needs no subsequent material, like the action that resolves the problem. A middle needs both prior and subsequent material, as does the entire interplay of needs and desires which can be presented in modal verbs.

The most sophisticated modern theorists seem to converge with Aristotle upon the observation that the plot of a successful literary work, and each of its component incidents, has this tripartite internal structure whose components may themselves be incidents or may be smaller units which lack this internal structure, just as oxygen or hydrogen lack the internal structure to be water.

7

But Siuzhets and the Incidents That Form Them Have Two Parts: An Expectation and Its Fulfillment or Frustration

If the finest modern experts agree with one another—and even with Aristotle—about a central point, it just has to be wrong.

And yet this tripartite identity for a plot and for the incidents arranged within it works excellently in describing the moves in a fairy tale and in dealing with other small literary forms like the stories in *The Decameron, The Arabian Nights,* or Sherlock Holmes. In such works, the siuzhet tracks the fabula very closely. Theoreticians of plot have long been worried, however, about the lyrical and reflective digressions of Gogol and Henry Fielding, or Don Quixote's long discussions of the nature of knighthood or of fantasy. These passages plainly lack the tripartite structure, yet they play important parts in two of the plot relationships we have enumerated: thematic association and narrative embedding. The Don explores chivalry in life and in theory. His embedded discourses may not be part of the fabula, but they interrupt our experience of it in the siuzhet, which lacks the tripartite structure that enables us to identify an incident and characterize a whole plot in the fabula.

The tripartite structure for an incident described in the previous chapter accounts for most literary practice in the fabula very well, but plot studies of larger forms have been less successful than those of smaller forms because incidents in the siuzhet actually have a bipartite structure that has received little attention. Rather than a situation, a need, and an action, such incidents in the siuzhet consist of an expectation and its fulfillment or frustration. As literary devices, suspense, surprise, and expectation belong primarily to the siuzhet, although characters can also experience them in harmony or in counterpoint with the reader: the chief person waiting for Godot is the reader or the member of the audience, and the power of Samuel Beckett's play resides in the nagging parallel between the reader's and the characters' expectations. A theorist in love with symmetry might argue that these incidents in the siuzhet are also tripartite; the central element, the need, resides not in the text but in the reader's need for the next page. E. M. Forster's distinction between plot and story is far less clear and useful than the one between fabula and siuzhet, but Forster caught this central fact about each incident in the siuzhet: "*Qua* story, it can only have one merit: that of making the audience want to know what happens next" (*Aspects of the Novel*, 47).

This sense that the siuzhet and each of the fractal elements within it create and respond to an expectation, while the fabula and its incidents build up through two steps to an action, concludes the theoretical part of this book.

Before turning to the two powerful works that occupy the rest of this study, let me play with my new toy for a moment and consider another small work of art: "The appearance of St. Gertrude to a nun of Poissy, in labor." I picked this incident because it is brief (you have just read it in its entirety) and because some of its relations are simple. In chapter 7 of the second book of François Rabelais's *Gargantua*, this is the title of one of the books in the library of St. Victor's. Like all too many books in our libraries today, this volume has no existence outside of the catalogue, and of all the literary subgenres, a catalogue can get away with paying the least attention to its fabula.

This incident has the internal structure of an incident in a fabula. A nun of Poissy is in labor; she needs help; the saint takes action and appears. Externally, this incident neither precedes nor follows nor is simultaneous with any other incident. If Rabelais had written a history, we would know that the saint had appeared before the assembly of the library, but in fiction, this chronological relationship is trivial. Spatially too, Poissy is related to some of the places in Rabelais on a map, but in the fictional plot it has no significant relationship. Catalogues exempt fictional incidents from the obligation to exist in the chronological and spatial system in which the characters in the rest of the novel exist, unless the author elects to mimic history and give up some of the freedoms fiction allows. Causally too, the actions of this nun and the saint neither cause nor result from any incident in the rest of the novel, including the catalogue. This achronism, atopism, and anaitism does not exempt the incident from other relations in the fabula. The pregnancy of the nun whose oath demands chastity subversively resembles the rough-and-ready role reversal of Rabelais's Friar John, whose religion demands pacifism and even occasional abstinence.

The siuzhet is more Rabelaisian: the first ten words in the English translation produce an expectation of prating piety. The last two words frustrate that expectation. The immediate neighbors of this incident offer no memorable contrast, parallel, or other tie with this title, although an ingenious critic can make any juxtaposition interesting. The incident is too brief to bracket another, and its place in the catalogue of books is more as a member than as an interruptor. The whole catalogue, of course, does act as an interruptor, a frequent role of catalogues since Homer's day.

The basic plot structures I have described can illuminate the simplest plot I could adduce for discussion. Perhaps they can offer some insights into two monumental works, *King Lear* and *Crime and Punishment*.

PART II

THE PLOT OF *KING LEAR* OPERATES PURPOSEFULLY BUT ALSO REFLECTS THE CREATIVE PROCESS

8

For Integrity of Impact, Stages, Actors, and the Audience Need a Unity of Action

Part 2 of this book locates the plot of *King Lear* theoretically and historically in the world of literary plots and then examines the plot in the light of certain critical reactions to it. This play has the magnitude and the idiosyncrasies to provoke and to test theoretical thinking. Aristotle thinks of tragedy as the representation of an action, the *mimesis* of a *praxis*. An "action" as he conceived it resembles what we have defined as a fabula, an expanded incident or a set of incidents organized in the world the characters inhabit, while the "representation" includes not only the siuzhet but also the five other constituent elements—character, diction, music, spectacle, and thought—which we have already referred to in the previous chapters. Dramatic plots, as Plato and Aristotle already knew, differ from epic plots because of certain basic differences between the genres. Although epics are often read aloud on public occasions and "closet" dramas may be designed for solitary reading, drama as a genre depends more on an audience sitting or standing together for a limited period and on actors impersonating characters on a stage. These characteristics make dramatic plots more direct and intense than those of epics or many other genres. Recognizing the power of plots combined with performance, Russian censors often permitted the publication but not the performance of plays they considered dangerous. Lyrics, still briefer, can have powerful plots, but they normally derive their central impact from other elements, such as diction, thought, and sometimes music.

Believing like Oscar Wilde that nature imitates art, that our lives enact what we read or watch, Plato concluded that literature—and drama especially—is therefore dangerous. But he also loved and honored literature: he constantly quoted Homer, Hesiod, the tragedians, and the lyricists; he wrote the most perceptive, powerful, and mythically rich prose in antiquity; and he advocated the use of fictions to motivate the citizens of his just state. To express this conflict between his fears and his proclivities, he confronts reason with emotion in a wonderful passage in the second and third books of *The Republic*. In this passage, Socrates gains agreement that in epic, lyric, or tragic plots the gods must do no harm and tell no lies (2.378) and that heroes must avoid any thought or action that might inspire cowardice, civil disobedience, or untimely laughter in an impressionable child or adult (3.387). He also worries that impersonating imperfect characters may corrupt an actor (3.396), but rather than instituting a censorship system, he proposes the following paradoxical behavior:

> We will fall down and worship [the poet] as a sweet and holy and wonderful being; but we must also inform him that in our State such as he are not permitted to exist. . . . And so, when we have anointed him with myrrh, and set a garland of wool upon his head, we shall send him away to another city.   (3.398)

Plato uses his highest and most moving literary art to banish literature from his just state. Censorship was plainly a troubling way to handle the conflict between the wonder and the danger that reside together in art.

Aristotle agreed with Plato—and with the fashionable American criticism of the 1970s—that most of our activities have goals that are political. In the 1970s, the word "political" became somewhat abstract at times; for Plato, abstractions were more real than things, but in this case, the word "political" relates concretely to the Greek city-state, the *polis*.

Aristotle agreed with his master that the well-being of the city was the proper goal of a citizen's activity, literary or otherwise. He was at least as deeply involved in literature and even more alert to the importance of imitation; yet he found a way to save literature in the service of the city-state, and the dramatic plot was his most powerful instrument for doing so. Plato had seen the audience in danger of imitating actions the poet had imitated weakly and inaccurately from a world that was itself a weak and inaccurate imitation of the "real" world of ideas. Aristotle simplifies the pattern: his poet imitates a reality that resides in the particular, not the abstraction, and the audience reacts to that imitation in two ways. First, it receives the satisfaction that comes from imitation itself, a satisfaction that little children and admirers of the Ashcan school of painting share with apes, who delight in aping even disgusting things, although Aristotle considers such imitation a strictly human activity. (This doctrine that art mimics nature has become so standard in the last two millennia that Wilde's enunciation of Plato's earlier doctrine is a good example of Wilde's most basic formula for wit: the naughty reversal of a truism.) Second, the audience reacts by purging itself of the emotions it has shared with the rest of the state in a great civic ceremony at the theater. Agreeing that terror and pity can lose battles and destroy cities if they spread among a citizenry and that laughter can make one less warlike, Aristotle circumvents Plato's fear that terror and pity might be habit-forming. Even though his ethics centers upon the idea of habituation, here Aristotle argues for a different principle: the idea that inoculation with these emotions under controlled conditions would protect the citizenry from their uncontrolled spread in a crisis. Aristotle calls the dramatic plot, or *mythos*, the chief source of terror, pity, and any other dangerous emotions that are useful in a drama, although character, reasoning, spectacle, music, or diction might optionally play a lesser role. With only a chorus, a few characters, a limited stage, and an hour or so of time, the tragedian must make the assembled audience experience terror and pity powerful enough to free them from these emotions in a real crisis. This goal and these limitations generate the classical rhetoric for drama. Virtually all Western students of drama accept these basic limitations of the genre. Even when the stage includes the entire Winter Palace Square, with thousands of characters in the cast and one heavy cruiser offshore, as it did in Nikolai

Evreinov's play about the 1917 revolution, or when a drama lasts for twelve hours, as does Robert Wilson's "opera" about Joseph Stalin, the staging is really a commentary on these limitations.

Even if it is to use character as well as plot—and Aristotle knew good tragedies that largely ignored character—it still must not seek to present a whole biography in a series of incidents that are related only because they involve the same person, but are not caused or affected by one another. A good epic may present a long series of related events, like Odysseus's experiences before and after his return to Ithaca, but a drama needs to imitate a single incident usually caused by an important string of causally related incidents and sometimes causing others, so as to imply the whole of the character's life.

This unity of action springs from the restrictions inherent in drama and exploits the special powers of drama. Epic, for example, offers quite different possibilities in plotting. To maximize the terror, pity, or other dangerous emotions of the audience, the action presented in a drama needs internal integrity more than it does in a less tightly restricted genre. The incidents selected must be causally connected.

Causality is unfashionable right now. I once scolded a rebellious adolescent for causing some damage, and he answered, "I'm not a causalist," disposing snappily of ten thousand years' work. But humanity derives as strong a pleasure from the perception of causation as it does from seeing imitation, perhaps for a similar, Darwinian reason. Creatures that understand cause and effect tend to survive, as do those that can imitate their parents' or community's example. In comedy, "I could see it coming" and "I didn't see it coming" are two causal epiphanies that bring pleasure quite independent of whether "it" matters at all. Buster Keaton may well be the grandmaster of causal humor in the twentieth century. When the entire side of a building falls on him, in one piece, a window opening lets the wall fall around him without touching him. Half the humor comes from Keaton's total failure to display the terror or the relief we experience, but the other half comes from the strict, geometrical logic that insists, like Denis Diderot's Jacques the Fatalist, that this happened this way and therefore had to happen this way. With no character present at all, Keaton could have one barrel in a freight car shift so as to dislodge another, whose movement makes another roll out the door, etc., so that nothing is going on but pure causation, and the movie audience cannot restrain its laughter.

Whatever his reasoning, Aristotle demanded that a dramatic plot be causally integrated and that any incident which can be omitted without breaking the causal sequence be omitted. This discipline in handling the causal relationship between incidents produces the sense of inevitability that characterizes the strongest tragedies. Oedipus struggles to avoid his destiny, but everything he does leads to it. This was no pedantic traditionalism, but a practice grounded on solid theory and clear observation of what worked within the undeniable limitations of drama in the West. A hero's entire life simply will not fit on stage, chronologically or spatially, but even a larger form, like epic, should not aspire to coverage. In epic, the standard is less vehement; incidents not indispensable to explain the next step may be introduced if they are causally connected, but unconnected incidents, even if they happen to the same character, detract from the artistic impact. Omitting some of Odysseus's encounters would impoverish the *Odyssey*, but its plot would remain intact. But Homer keeps his invention of the Trojan horse, his deceit of Philoctetes, and Odysseus's other exploits outside the causal system of the epic. As the pedants turned Aristotle's practical observations about successful plays into Hellenistic or neoclassical rules, this unity of action slopped over into the three classical unities: first, the unity of space, ideally confining the displayed action to a single courtyard, street corner, or other place no bigger than a stage, but permitting an expansion as far as the city walls if the action demanded it. Second, for time, the ideal limit is the amount of time the play took to present, but Aristotle himself had mentioned that this might expand to twenty-four hours, or even a little more (*Poetics*, 49b). The unity of action is the central matter, but it is harder to establish without a serious understanding of the causal relationships in the fabula of the play. Canto 3 of Nicolas Boileau-Despréaux's *The Art of Poetry* (*L'Art poétique*) makes these rules a matter of reason and of commercial success:

> But we on whom Reason imposes its rule
> Desire that the Plot be Arranged with art's grace,
> A single Deed done in one time and one Place,
> Right up to the ending to hold the seats full.   (43)

Many theorists justified these limits in terms of verisimilitude—the audience cannot believe that a street becomes a forest, or that minutes represent days—but Aristotle's more pragmatic mind was more involved with the integrity of impact, the capacity to produce and thereby purge the emotions Plato had felt forced to censor.

9

Shakespeare Replaced the Greek Unity of Action with a New Thematic Unity Based on Parallelism

The Shakespearean plot departs from the classical plot in ways that relate to the conditions of performance, the dramatic tradition, and the author. The Greek state provided the chorus, actors, and enormous theater to stage a ceremony before the honored judges in the front row. Shakespeare's most challenging judges were also in the front row, but they were the rowdy standees in a crowded commercial theater or, occasionally, the dangerous egos of the Renaissance court. Sophocles's audience often saw three or four plays in a single afternoon, while Shakespeare's audience normally saw just one. It took a professional actor like Shakespeare to elaborate out of the classical and other traditions he inherited a kind of drama that could control such an audience for hours.

Stendhal's article on Racine and Shakespeare concentrates on only two of the classical unities: "The whole dispute between Racine and Shakespeare can be reduced to learning whether observing the two unities of place and time allow one to make plays of lively interest to nineteenth-century spectators, plays that make them weep and tremble" (*Oeuvres completes*, 12). Stendhal's omission of the unity of action here may throw more light on his style of argumentation than on his theatrical beliefs. Certainly Aristotle devoted far more attention to the unity of action than to those of place or time, though Boileau-Despréaux compressed the three into a single line as if they mattered equally. Stendhal proceeds to defend Shakespeare by disputing the verisimilitude of the two unities, arguing that it is no harder to believe that ten minutes represents a year than a day, which Aristotle himself had allowed (*Poetics*, 49b1.W1). This psychology of verisimilitude does not apply to the unity of action; a tightly linked causal system is neither more nor less likely than a series of causally unrelated incidents, and therefore has nothing to do with the particular weakness Stendhal finds in the classical doctrine that required observation of the unities. Aristotle's more philosophical doctrine of verisimilitude has little to do with likelihood and is related to the unity of action. For example, Aristotle praises the plot in which the statue of Mitis fell on the man who caused Mitis's death, killing him (52a9). Such an event is far less likely than being killed by a random falling object, as Aeschylus was when a seagull tried to crack a turtle's shell by dropping it on his bald head, which in itself is a rare enough event. The falling statue seems not to happen at random and avoids the episodic plot, where there is neither probability nor necessity that the episodes follow one another. Probability here is not a matter of statistics, but the sense of living in an orderly universe. Aristotle carries this reasoning all the way in his *Poetics*, preferring certain impossible incidents as more probable than certain incidents that had actually occurred but lacked this verisimilitude (60a27). Stendhal prefers to attack the pedants and ignore the important fact that, in most of his plays, Shakespeare ignores the unity of action.

The argument for a causally integrated plot is important, as suggested in the previous chapter, and even though he had "small Latin and less Greek," Shakespeare must have known this, whether directly or indirectly. Shakespeare needed a real reason to give up a perfectly sound dramatic practice for one relatively untried by major dramatists. He sacrificed the causal tightness that had served classic drama so well in order to build thematic tightness around parallel plots. Usually the parallel plots involve different social levels—masters and servants, kings and courtiers, supernatural beings and humans—and usually the plots are not too parallel to intersect occasionally and interact causally at some level, though never enough to satisfy Aristotle's criterion that if any incident be removed, the whole plot of the play should cease to make sense. If the Earl of Gloucester should be removed from *King Lear,* the plot involving the king and his daughters would hardly be affected, except for the very end, where Gloucester's son Edmund is responsible for the deaths of the three daughters. Shakespeare sacrifices the tight integrity of the causal relationships between incidents in order to explore the parallels between two sets of incidents, provoking our awareness of the common elements. For Aristotle, a causal connection did not need to be real to bear verisimilitude; it needed to make the universe look well organized. For Shakespeare, this same effect could emerge from incidents linked not by causality or false causality that seems real, but by similarity.

Similarity and difference can be treated in many ways. They involve adjectives that can be applied to discrete things, but philosophers can dispute whether the adjectives represent qualities that actually inhere in those things or whether we project them upon those things, and indeed, whether any two things are discrete or whether we project their separate identity upon a fuzzy or a nonexistent world. I know of a child who complained about her first pair of glasses that all they did was put lines around people. Michel de Montaigne said that if all men were not different, we could not tell them apart, and if they were not all similar we could not tell them from dogs; something similar can be said about any pair of Shakespearian plots or incidents. When I walk along the street without my glasses, I cannot always recognize my friends, but as compensation, I sometimes nod politely to people I have never seen before. The ability to see similarity is very hard to tell from the inability to see difference. The person I embarrass with my greeting may genuinely resemble some friend of mine in some key features, and my myopia keeps me from noticing the remaining features. In the same way, perhaps I distinguish the friend I fail to greet from himself because of my extraordinary lack of acuity. But in comparing these people or the double plots of a Shakespeare play, the key features exist in my own mind, though constantly tested against the appearance of my friends or the dramatic text. We have already mentioned the doctrine in pattern-recognition that everything has some common features with everything else and that no two things are either identical or different in all ways.

In literature, some of these problems disappear because, as Philip Sidney said, poesy claims not to be true, and some of the similarity has only literary existence. The same patterns apply, however, in literature, and when we say, "It's a bird! It's a plane! It's Superman!" or "It was not a flock of swans.... It was the ten fingers of Boyan on the strings"; the possibility of mistaking a man for a plane or a bard's hands for gorgeous-voiced birds descending shows us how Superman flies and Boyan sings and plays, just as a simile would. Similarity in plots can be represented as the overlap between two areas, and those areas may be broken down into individual points of similarity, dissimilarity, contrast, etc. Without knowing it, a Shakespearean audience is making such analyses all the time it watches a play, and the points of overlap and contrast enter their awareness.

Similarities between characters are only a secondary subject for this book, but similarities between two roles are part of the relationship among the incidents, that is, of the plot. In *Henry IV, Part I*, Shakespeare constructs a plot about three competing excellences: the wit and fellowship of Falstaff's world in Eastcheap; the gallantry and poetry of Hotspur in London and the north and west of Britain; and the royal purposefulness of Henry IV at his court and encampment. Each of these worlds derides or decries the other two, and each has its own weaknesses: Falstaff's criminality, drunkenness, and cowardice; Hotspur's reckless lack of self-control; and King Henry's edgy status as a usurper. Prince Hal confronts all three, entering into each world—wittily into that of Falstaff, gallantly into that of Hotspur, and calculatingly and perhaps a little pompously into that of the king. Near the end, he stands between the prostrate bodies of Hotspur and Falstaff and bids them both farewell. The causal connections among the three plots are tenuous, but the three role models illuminate each other, and Hal's conspiracy to rob Falstaff the thief parodies Hotspur's conspiracy to depose King Henry, the usurper, since each role model resists having done unto himself what he has done unto others.

10

Shakespeare Uses Conflict, the Righting of Wrongs, the Healing of an Inruption or Disruption, and Other Standard Plotting Devices, But His Recognition Scenes Move Us Most

Theorists tend to agree about the limitations that characterize drama in the West, but they differ about its social goals. Some follow Aristotle's argument that it is cathartic, others agree with Plato that it is exemplary, and many modern critics tend to claim that the shared dramatic experience itself is the chief social justification. Most theorists accept all three goals but tend to foreground one of them. These differences over goals shape the key moments of the play, when the audience is suddenly moved to tears, terror, laughter, or other big emotions. These climactic moments in a play seem to take three basic forms, as described by classical, nineteenth-, and twentieth-century critics. The first to be named is also the most striking and powerful: the recognition scene that reveals a person's nature, identity, or situation, correcting either an error or a lie. The second is the scene of repentance, forgiveness, or other reconciliation, healing a conflict or restoring the equilibrium after an inruption into or disruption of a previously stable world. The third is the *scène à faire*, the righting a wrong, the punishing or scolding a villain, or making justice triumph in such a way as to unify an audience in its shared satisfaction at the outcome. The strongest dramas, and some weak ones, tend to use all three kinds of climax, exploiting our shared thirst for truth, security, and justice. These are not the only moments when the plot suddenly moves the audience to tears or terror or laughter, but other key moments tend to operate on a smaller scale. These include scenes of extraordinary fidelity, often by servants or family members who sacrifice all they have to save their lord or loved one. A related type of scene displays extraordinary and often unwarranted generosity, and a third, the stubborn assertion of one's will despite inevitable consequent pain. These may also be combined with the climactic scenes or with one another.

A recognition scene needs a lie or an error. A reconciliation scene needs conflict. A *scène à faire* needs a villain, big or small. It has been claimed that the three most important elements in a dramatic plot are conflict, conflict, and conflict. Aristotle has little to say about conflict because the Greeks took it for granted. Greek theatrical practice tended to revolve around the *agon*, or the struggle between a protagonist and his or her antagonist. Sometimes, one of the two is good and the other evil, but often villainy remains ambiguous. Later classical drama often locates the struggle between good and evil inside a character, although the two moral drives may have representatives in the cast of characters. The conflict may take place between competing characters or competing values that are equally good or evil, such as love and duty. Even then, the hero may hover between two characters representing different sets of values, as Neoptolemus does between Philoctetes and Odysseus, so that the abstract internal conflict can be represented on stage. Usually, the conflict erupts between human beings possessing different kinds of power. In *Oedipus at Colonus*, Creon possesses political and military power while Oedipus possesses the chthonic power of mysterious prophecies and of the deep taboos that he has broken, as well as the nasty personal power of vindictive old age. In *Oedipus the King*, the comparable conflict between the able king and the authoritative old priest drives only a part of the plot; the rest represents the conflict between Oedipus and the destiny he has been warned about.

The presence of a conflict produces suspense as to its outcome, and it often involves the audience on one side or the other as the conflict moves toward a climax. The end of a conflict may be a triumph of some representative of the status quo, of the underdog, or of some other figure, but the sequel to it is normally a reconciliation of some sort. Once

Claudius is dead, Hamlet can forgive Laertes, and Fortinbras can restore the equilibrium that was destroyed by the inruption of the students from Wittenberg and the murder of two kings, though it is restored at a reduced and saddened level. At the end of Plautus's *Menaechmi*, the young lovers and the villainous whoremaster go off to dinner together. An Aristotelian reading treats this ending as the aftermath of catharsis, while a Platonist in our terms will regard it as a model for behavior, involving the audience in the reconstruction of the polity.

For many modern theorists of drama, this audience involvement constitutes not a means, but an end. The play exists not to purge the society of undesirable emotions, nor yet to educate the audience in desirable ones, but to provide a moment of solidarity in a shared vicarious experience at a great ceremony. In the commercial theatre of the nineteenth century, the center of the plot was often not primarily a conflict but, as in the fairy tales Propp studied, an injustice or other wrong, and the central moment was the *scène à faire*, the moment when the villain received their comeuppance or the hero or heroine told the villain off. This moment was justified not by the needs of the polity or those of society, but by the shared desires of the individual members of the audience. Eugène Scribe's *scène à faire* would often show the villain's ruin, but the satisfaction it gave outweighed any terror or pity, and civic usefulness played little part in the author's plan. Jerzy Grotowski and a number of the finest theatrical minds of the twentieth century have adopted this ideal of the theatrical as an end in itself, constructing their productions in an avant-garde variant of the nineteenth-century melodrama, with the audience as moral or immoral participants in the action rather than its spectacle.

Let us look last at recognition scenes. The concern with terror and pity that have long shaped our discussions may have originated in Aristotle's departure from Plato over the dangers of drama, but it took on a life of its own in the *Poetics* and helped Aristotle give a name to a pattern that has characterized most of the most successful tragedies and comedies in Western culture ever since: the recognition scene that causes or discloses a reversal in the fortunes of the hero. For Aristotle's mind, the most exciting experience in life was probably what the Gestalt psychologists called an "aha": the moment when a body of data or experience suddenly shifts from incomprehensibility or from an incorrect and unsatisfactory understanding to something that clearly makes sense. This experience matches what Aristotle sought in a recognition scene and is not far from his definition of happiness in the *Ethics* (1177b). Shakespeare was as Aristotelian in this respect as the ancient tragedians, using the same technique to produce terror, pity, and, in comedy, laughter.

The recognition must take place in the mind of a character in the drama, but it may or may not also take place in the minds of the audience. If the audience knows what one or more characters do not, the audience experiences the powerful effect of dramatic irony. If the audience does not know, it experiences its own "aha," rather than a vicarious one. Both systems work well, and as Aristotle himself pointed out, in some cases a small part of the audience experiences dramatic irony, while the majority do not know the myth that forms the basis for a play and experiences the same "aha" as the hero. In the *Iphigenia in Tauris*, until Iphigenia identifies her brother whom she is about to sacrifice, only the goddess Aphrodite shares the audience's knowledge. In *Philoctetes*, Odysseus's elaborate falsehood about Neoptolemus's mission makes the audience and Neoptolemus squirm when Philoctetes trusts him, and fills the recognition scene with terror and pity that the audience shares with Neoptolemus. Both these recognition scenes are preceded at first by *curiosité* and then by suspense, as the audience comes to realize the impending horror, which in these two plays is averted by a god winched down to the stage, since classical tragedy did not depend on an unhappy outcome.

Shakespeare's predilection for recognition scenes peaks in the fifth scene of the fifth act of *Cymbeline*, a play whose plot has attracted little praise over the centuries, though the play's beauty can move us deeply. The scene opens with ten bewildered characters on stage. Five of them are disguised, standing around awaiting royal, mutual, and, in two cases, self-recognition scenes. Not recognizing them after many years, Cymbeline rewards his own now grown sons and their abductor for turning the tide of a battle and saving England, regretting at the same time the absence of their co-fighter, whom the audience knows to be Posthumus, the son-in-law he had exiled. The first recognition, oddly enough, involves none of the disguised figures. It comes in the classical tradition, with a report that Cymbeline's queen has died, confessing that she had planned to poison Cymbeline and his daughter, Imogen. The king's recognition of his uxorious delusion gives this moment some of the gratifying quality of a *scène à faire*, but his justification of his blindness ends with self-reproach and a prayer:

> Mine eyes
> Were not at fault, for she was beautiful;
> Mine ears, that heard her flattery; nor my heart,
> That thought her like her seeming. It had been vicious
> To have mistrusted her. Yet, (O my daughter!)
> That it was folly in me thou mayst say
> And prove it in thy feeling. Heaven mend all!
>
> (5.5.62–68)

This moment leaves Shakespeare with a dozen recognitions and less than four hundred lines to go. But he takes his time. Cymbeline half-recognizes his daughter, dressed as a page: "His favor is familiar to me. Boy, / thou hast looked thyself into my grace / and art mine own" (5.5.93–95). But Imogen has recognized the Machiavellian villain Iachimo among a group of captives and, in a great reversal, has power over him through the king. Iachimo confesses on stage, and it costs Shakespeare many more lines than the queen's reported confession. The disguised Posthumus, listening, realizes that he has ordered his wife to be killed for a fabricated adultery. His outburst leads all hands to recognize him and his hysterical attack unveils Imogen, forcing the doctor to admit to deceiving the evil queen and several others by substituting sleeping medicine for the deadly poison she had ordered. Shakespeare slips into narration to generate several further recognitions, but the emotional center of the scene shifts from recognition to reconciliation. Posthumus embraces his wife in answer to her tender reproach, saying, "Hang there like fruit, my soul, / till the tree die" (5.5.263–64). And the king has said, "If this be so, the Gods do mean to strike me / to death with mortal joy" (5.5.234–35), and finally realizes that it is so: "How now, my flesh, my child? / What, mak'st thou me a dullard in this act? / Wilt thou not speak to me?" (5.5.264–66). When she requests his blessing, he answers, "My tears that fall / prove holy water on thee" (5.5.268–69). Almost unimaginably in such a tangle, these tears prove contagious, and a good actor can make his listeners weep. The reconciliations even include a pardon for Iachimo and a peace with the Roman Empire.

In this way, Shakespeare uses all three kinds of climax, prepared for throughout the play, and gives up any semblance of unity. Shakespeare, if anyone ever understood it, knew and treasured the dramatic in drama, but more than a third of this scene is narrative. Narrative is commonplace at the beginning of a play to lay out the opening situation and at the end to divulge crucial secrets to the audience or to avoid having too many corpses lying around the stage, but this narration is entirely about matters that the audience has seen in the past hour or two. Scholars have argued that Shakespeare was simply experimenting with a new style, the dramatic romance, which he only mastered in *The Tempest*. One could argue that *The Tempest* works well on stage, while in *Cymbeline* the complexities are too numerous. This final scene suggests something else. It is an epilogue, a genre that forms an important part of nineteenth-century novels and certain other genres, but is hardly necessary in a play. In the Romantic period major poets often switched to novels. Walter Scott, Victor Hugo, and, to some extent, Goethe did, and Pushkin and Mikhail Lermontov were moving in that direction when their careers were cut short. Shakespeare knew many novellas and novels and romances—classical, medieval, and Renaissance—but he had no fully developed novelistic models. He was working on *Pericles* in the same years as *Cymbeline*, and *Pericles* is closer to Greek romance than any other Shakespearean play. I would claim that Shakespeare, having created the central canon for the English sonnet and the central canon for English comedy and tragedy—history plays having been in place before him—was preparing himself to invent the modern English novel when he was cut off by death. Part 3 of this book will deal with novelistic plots, but here it will suffice to say that if Shakespeare had lived as long as Tolstoy did, he might have read Cervantes, and the modern novel would have begun in England, rather than in France or Spain.

II

Shakespeare Prepares for His Recognition Scenes with Elaborate Lies

Shakespeare was willing to sacrifice the unity of action to achieve the richness of implication that resides in the presence of more than one plot, but Stendhal was certainly wrong on the first pages of his *Racine and Shakespeare* to reduce the conflict between Shakespearian and classical tragedy to the abandonment of the unities. In this chapter, I would like to concentrate on a little-discussed peculiarity of Shakespearean plotting, the use of lies. We have discussed recognition scenes as key moments in the production of terror, pity, or laughter and have said that the stage is set for such scenes by errors or lies. In the surviving classical dramas, these two ways of complicating the plot are about equally prevalent. In Shakespeare's comedies and tragedies, except in a single play, which is carefully labeled, virtually every recognition scene is generated primarily out of a lie, not an error.

Shakespeare may have had several reasons for preferring lies to errors as an instrument for complicating his plots: most simply, lying is a wonderful activity. It excels factuality because it is unrestricted by the limits of possibility, and excels fiction as well because it claims to be true; it is as creative as sex and is as human as you are, but endlessly richer. Plausible lying demands skill, ingenuity, psychological insight, and a capacity for consistency and coherence worthy of an epic or dramatic poet, but the rewards for really splendid lies are greater, for both the liar and the person lied to. In chapter 9 of his *Tale of a Tub*, Jonathan Swift called this "the sublime and refined point of felicity ..., the possession of being well deceived" (84), and Nietzsche's *Will to Power* links it with both art and love: "When a man loves, he is a good liar about himself, and to himself; he seems to himself transfigured, stronger, richer, more perfect; he is more perfect.... Art here acts as an organic function; we find it present in the most angelic instinct, 'love'; we find it as the greatest stimulus of life—thus art is sublimely utilitarian even in the fact that it lies" (426–27 [4.4.808]). And Benjamin N. Cardozo is really talking about lies, not fictions, when he says, "Law has built up many of its doctrines by a make-believe that things are other than they are, ... a class of fictions ... which is a working tool of thought, but which at times hides itself from view till reflection and analysis have brought it to the light" (*The Paradoxes of Legal Science*, 34). If art and love and law all rest on lies, we have begun dealing with one of humanity's most beneficial and unappreciated activities. In fact, we might take very seriously the remark of Razumikhin, the Dostoevsky character most like Dostoevsky: "I am human because I lie" (*Crime and Punishment*, pt. 3, chap. 1). The argument can be made that a human being can make only one statement that is undeniable and unquestionable. No one can say "I am," or "I am not," or "I know," or "I know not," or "I cogitate," or "Atoms fall in space," or "God is omnipotent," or "God is good," or "God is dead," or "Good and evil strive," or "I have will," or any other thing without arousing doubts in one quarter or another. But one rock we can stand upon beyond all questioning: "I am a liar."

This valorization of lying applies to a rather simple kind of lie, a statement the liar knows to be untrue. This definition excludes self-deception, which is another topic, and ignores the question of whether the liar is correct about untruth. Deluded characters may state something true and still be liars if they believe it to be untrue. This definition also tends to ignore what Harry Frankfurt's book defines as bullshit, the blithe unconcern about whether one's statement is true or not. Most lies involve three people: the liar, the person lied to, and the person (or, occasionally, the thing) lied about. These roles may merge, as when Falstaff lies about how he himself behaved in a battle or a robbery, or when Sir

Toby persuades Malvolio that he is most attractive in cross garters. In Shakespeare, lies may be self-serving or they may be altruistic, designed to help the person lied to or the one lied about, or someone else. They may be vicious, designed to harm others or even oneself, as when Julia in *The Two Gentlemen of Verona* denies her feelings, tears up a love letter, and says to herself, "O hateful hands, to tear such loving words" (1.2.105). These lies often miscarry in their intent, as Friar Laurence's lie about Juliet's death does in its design to help Romeo and Juliet, but the lie about Hero's death arranged by Friar Francis in *Much Ado about Nothing* works beautifully. Surprisingly often, the lie is revelatory, expressing facts about the liar, the person lied to, or the person lied about.

But this varied array of uses for lies should not obscure a more professional reason for Shakespeare to introduce so many of them into his plays. In a way, each lie is a little drama, with at least the rudiments of a plot, and many of Shakespeare's plays center on big lies where one person or a group of conspirators entrain others into a play within a play. In *Hamlet* and the introduction to *The Taming of the Shrew*, the lord arranges for a group of professional actors to perform a play to manipulate one person in the audience. In *Love's Labor's Lost*, *A Midsummer Night's Dream*, *The Merry Wives of Windsor*, and *The Tempest*, local groups stage elaborate outdoor performances, one to tease and torture Falstaff and the other three for the delectation of the stage audience. But in all six of these plays, there is a second play within the play: the leader also orders, manipulates, or persuades others to carry out an elaborate plot to bring his will to bear on one character (or in *The Tempest*, two). Shakespeare uses many other such puppet-masters or theatrical directors who do not call the performances they arrange dramas and who use the characters around them, sometimes with the connivance of others, sometimes by lying to everybody. Launce in *The Two Gentlemen of Verona* may be the kindest of these liars when he confesses to befouling the floor in order to avert a beating of his dog, who had done so. At the other end of the spectrum, Iago is the most evil of the puppet-masters, making Cassio his unwitting accomplice and Amelia his half-understanding helper, and Desdemona and Othello themselves not only victims but participants in the drama he concocts. Iago's drama has only Othello's destruction as its goal, no personal gain. In *Measure for Measure* an equally elaborate set of lies by the Duke is benevolent. He uses his absence, his disguise, and Isabel and Mariana's identities in the hope of reforming Vienna and, later, of thwarting Angelo's own elaborated lies. When disguises transform women into men, who are often seeking a rapprochement with the men they love, as Julia does in *The Two Gentlemen of Verona*, Rosalind in *As You Like It*, Viola in *Twelfth Night*, Portia in *The Merchant of Venice*, or Imogen in *Cymbeline*, these britches parts are all revelatory. Since on the Shakespearean stage all these women's parts were played by boys, the disguises restored the actors to their own gender.

Many of the lies in Shakespeare are intended to be revealed in a recognition scene, like that where Hal reveals that he and Poins have robbed Falstaff or where Prospero reunites the lost in *The Tempest*. Sometimes they are designed never to be believed in the first place, as on the sunny day when Petruchio says, "I say it is the moon that shines so bright," simply to assert his will (*The Taming of the Shrew*, 4.5.4). If such lies are taken seriously, like the flattery of the toadies in *Timon of Athens*, the liars are nonplussed. More often, the liar intends the lie to go undiscovered, but in Shakespeare, it never does, although unrevealed lies can be very serviceable dramatically, as in Ferenc Molnár's *The Play's the Thing*.

Shakespeare's minor characters lie handsomely and with enough variety to constitute an encyclopedia of the resources of lying, but in this chapter, the larger lies that lead to the main recognition scenes are of more interest. These lies can expand the classical dramatic form that the Elizabethans inherited, but the Greeks already used extensive additional plots embedded within the main plot by the liar, using containment to relate it back to the main plot. Sophocles embedded a second plot in the *Philoctetes* with Odysseus's lies, and Euripides as well in *Iphigenia at Aulis* with Agamemnon's lying, so the Elizabethans had this tradition to build on. In Shakespeare, these elaborated lies take on lives of their own and introduce alternative plots into the dramas, expanding them much as Homeric similes expand into vignettes of life or nature far from the action of the epic.

Of the dozen recognition scenes we discussed in *Cymbeline*, only one grew out of an error: Imogen mistook the dastard Cloten's headless body for her husband's. Cloten had worn Posthumus's clothes not to deceive but to spite Imogen, so she makes an error untouched by lies. This pure error is a rarity in Shakespeare. In *Twelfth Night* and the carefully labeled *Comedy of Errors*, Shakespeare has a pair of siblings each believe the other has been drowned in a shipwreck, and recycles a variant of the conceit in *Pericles*, but the rest of his dozens of recognitions all correct lies.

12

In *King Lear*, Shakespeare Uses Elaborated Lies to Psychologize the Gloucester Subplot

The plot of *King Lear* unites the plot of the old king and his three daughters with that of the Earl of Gloucester and his two sons. The two plots occupy the same space and time: the court of the aging Lear and his family, the countryside around, and much of pagan England. Causally, the two are loosely linked. If Lear and his family had not existed, Edmund's lechery, gallantry, and Machiavellian skill would have had less free play. Edmund is directly or indirectly responsible for the death of Lear's three daughters, but Lear and Gloucester have little impact on one another, and their destinies are determined primarily by their own children. To use Aristotle's test, either plot could have been omitted without radically altering the other. The play contains many brief narrations, but neither plot is significantly embedded in the other, so that the chief relationship between the two plots is (typically for Shakespeare) in the world of parallelism and contrast.

The symmetries are constructed to confront the audience with two old sinners whose wicked children play on their overwhelming credulity to gain their property and then destroy them, despite the self-sacrificing efforts of their faithful, loving children. The contrasts are almost as obvious: king vs. earl, daughters vs. sons, madness vs. blindness, etc., but this chapter will center on the magnitude of the lies used to set the plots in motion. Lear's evil daughters proclaim their love for their father in some of the most beautiful language Shakespeare ever wrote:

> Sir, I love you more than word can wield the matter
> Dearer than eyesight, space, and liberty;
> Beyond what can be valuèd, rich or rare;
> No less than life, with grace, health, beauty, honor;
> As much as child e'er loved, or father found;
> Beyond all manner of so much I love you.　　(I.I.36–42)

Goneril's speech is a lie, a contradiction of her real feelings. It turns out to be important, but is elaborate only in the gorgeousness of its diction, not for any plot embedded in it. Cordelia's contrasting speech does have the rudiments of a plot:

> I love your Majesty
> According to my bond; no more nor less.
> . . . .
> You have begot me, bred me, loved me; I
> Return those duties back as are right fit,
> Obey you, love you, and most honour you.
> Haply, when I shall wed,
> That lord whose hand must take my plight shall carry
> Half my love with him, half my care and duty.
> Sure I shall never marry like my sisters,
> To love my father all.　　(I.I.74–75, 79–87)

Cordelia does love Lear and obeys his banishment order, but her way of honoring him is unusual, and she goes far beyond her filial duties when she risks her royal life with her husband and dies trying to save her father. It may not be a striking lie; like Edgar lying to Gloucester, she hopes to shock her father back into the truth, but the untruth her lie narrates is revealing. Cordelia's lie contains a situation, a need, and an action—marriage—which has a result that could become the basis of further steps in an embedded plot, but as a speech it is primarily an unsuccessful antidote to the speeches of her villainous sisters, who lie in the standard manner of court flatterers, almost as a matter of course. (When asked how to deal with Queen Victoria, Prime Minister Benjamin Disraeli answered, "Lay it on with a trowel.") If Lear had known himself less slenderly, he would have ignored the false statements of all three daughters, or not solicited them in the first place. In the next scene, Shakespeare wants us to compare Edmund's lie with Goneril's and Regan's acquisitive speeches, but also with Cordelia's precipitating lie. Both Edmund and Cordelia answer their fathers, "Nothing, my lord" and generate an interchange on nothing, but Edmund, the son, instigates one crisis, with Gloucester responding to his lies, while Lear instigates the other, with his daughters responding with lies. Cordelia's lie has a rudimentary plot; Edmund stages a whole play within the Gloucester plot. Edmund invents a parricidal plot and tricks his brother into playing a plausible villain's role. His lie gradually co-opts the whole apparatus of the state into the pursuit of his brother and eventually his father.

Psychologically, Edmund's lie has classical Freudian implications. This drama of parricide by Edgar that Edmund has embedded in *King Lear* is the instrument of the parricide he himself is attempting. He wounds his own arm to make his lie more persuasive, but at a deeper level his lecherous impulsiveness parallels that of the lecherous father he is punishing for the good sport at begetting him; the wound punishes both generations, just as his lie about his pain at denouncing his father—"O heavens! that this treason were not, or not I the detector!" (3.5.12–13)—serves a practical purpose but also reflects some level of genuine horror at his greedy destruction of the father who begot him. In his pre-Soviet years, Konstantin Stanislavsky believed that an actor playing a villain should always seek out the villain's virtues and foreground them. Edmund is a magnificent playwright and has composed a great role for himself: reluctant fidelity to Gloucester and then the same to Cornwall that is painful because it goes against his flesh and blood. He uses other lies for other purposes: simultaneous betrothal to Goneril and Regan for sensuality and the joy of deceiving husbands and concealment of his orders to kill Lear and Cordelia as a way to let the murder happen unimpeded. But these less elaborate lies are instruments for gaining ends, and only secondarily ways of expressing his own identity and those of other characters.

His brother Edgar, whom he has accused of attempting Gloucester's murder, concocts lies that are even more elaborate. To escape pursuit, he takes it into his head:

> To take the basest and most poorest shape
> That ever penury, in contempt of man,
> Brought near to beast. My face I'll grime with filth,
> And with presented nakedness outface
> The winds and persecutions of the sky.
> The country gives me proof and precedent
> Of Bedlam beggars, who, with roaring voices,
> Strike in their numb'd and mortified bare arms
> Pins, wooden pricks, nails, sprigs of rosemary.
>
> (2.3.4–16)

This pattern of self-mutilation in the arm seems to run in the family, but Edgar has chosen a role for himself that is the very opposite of his brother's, one that is base and self-mortifying rather than noble and surprised by an assailant. His lie takes on a biographical identity:

> A serving-man, proud in heart and mind, that curl'd my hair,
> wore gloves in my cap, serv'd the lust of
> my mistress' heart and did the act of darkness with
> her; swore as many oaths as I spake words,
> and broke them in the sweet face of heaven; one that
> slept in the contriving of lust, and wak'd to do it.
> Wine lov'd I deeply, dice dearly, and in woman
> out-paramour'd the Turk.   (3.4.85–92)

Edgar's description of his current diet—frogs, toads, tadpoles, wall-newts, rats, and mice—enriches this social and sexual self-abasement in ways that demand more explanation than the plot of his brother's lies does.

For Edgar, this is only the first disguise. While guiding his blinded father, he changes his clothes and seems to speak better. He takes him to the imaginary cliff, describes the dizzy height, and tells the audience, "Why I do trifle thus with his despair / is done to cure it," but then adds,

"And yet I know not how conceit [imagination] may rob / the treasury of life when life itself / yields to the theft" (4.6.33-34, 42-44). In short, he risks killing his father with an enormously elaborated lie in order to cure him, but the plot of the lie he uses embeds his father's melodramatic suicide attempt in the plot of the play. This leads to two more disguises for Edgar. He impersonates a passerby who describes the figure Gloucester left at the top of the cliff: "His eyes / Were two full moons; He had a thousand noses, / Horns whelk'd and wav'd like the enridgèd sea: / It was some fiend" (4.6.69-72). Edgar continues to select unprepossessing guises for himself—in this last case, a demon. Edgar's new lie, less plausible than Edmund's but still appealing to his father's superstitious streak, continues to endanger Gloucester's life, as Edgar himself admits later on: "Became his guide, / led him, begg'd for him, sav'd him from despair; / never, (O fault!) reveal'd myself to him / until some half hour past" (5.3.191-94). The fault he realizes too late is simply that he, not his brother Edmund, kills his father. The weapon is the most powerful instrument in Shakespeare's armamentarium, a recognition scene:

> Not sure, though hoping of this good success,
> I ask'd his blessing, and from first to last
> Told him my pilgrimage. But his flaw'd heart,
> Alack, too weak the conflict to support!
> Twixt two extremes of passion, joy and grief,
> Burst smilingly.   (5.3.195-200)

This recognition scene is recounted in a long narrative in the final recognition scene in *King Lear*. It plays an active role in the causal system, motivating Edmund's revelation of his writ on Lear's and Cordelia's lives, in spite of his own nature. The Earl of Gloucester is the center of the three plots—Edmund's lie, Edgar's lie, and Shakespeare's fiction—in which the two false plots are embedded. In Edmund's lies, Edgar plans Gloucester's death, attacks Edmund, and escapes to help Lear. In Edgar's lies, a madman obsessed with demons or a demon itself assists Gloucester's suicide attempt, which fails because he has become as light as gossamer and floated down the cliff at Dover. In Shakespeare's lies, the Duke of Cornwall puts Gloucester's eyes out for helping Lear, and Gloucester's son Edgar leads him across England and makes two efforts to kill him, the second of which succeeds. The two lies and the presented version are incompatible with respect to Gloucester, but curiously Edmund's lie and Edgar's depiction of himself as a demon or madman are quite compatible with the way Edgar torments and eventually kills Gloucester. Edgar's devotion is real, but his lies are cruel, to both his father and himself. He is operating in a world of anger that comes out in his speech to his dying brother about their father, who was less than half an hour dead: "The gods are just, and of our pleasant vices/ Make instruments to scourge us. / The dark and vicious place where thee he got / Cost him his eyes." (5.3.171–74).

Edgar bottles up his rage, but displays it in the plots of his lies, which never deal with Edmund. Edmund's lies turn Edgar's hidden feelings into plans and intentions. Both brothers wound their arms to confirm their lies, but also, at some level, to punish their own aggressiveness.

If the Lear plot and the Gloucester plot of the play are parallel, this light on Edgar's motives should throw some light on Cordelia's. But here, the play fails to crystallize. The Lear plot contains no great Machiavellian lies that entrain others in the deception and move from step to step like Edmund's and Edgar's. In fact, the absence of certain lies from the Lear plot deserves special attention.

13

Tolstoy and Tate Preferred the Comforting Plots of *Lear*'s Sources to Shakespeare's, But Shakespeare Had Considered That Variant and Rejected It

The *King Lear* plot came to Shakespeare from three main sources: *Holinshed's Chronicles*, Edmund Spenser's *Faerie Queene*, and an earlier play, *The True Chronicle History of King Leir*. In all three accounts, Lear and Cordelia survive the events; the horror of the ending is Shakespeare's own. Tolstoy detested this plot and everything else about *King Lear*. He is not customarily included in the canon of great humorists, but his six-thousand-word narration of *King Lear* is, as translators in the Slavic field sometimes say, genial.

His summary of certain passages is masterful: when Lear brings Cordelia's body on stage, crying:

> Howl, howl, howl! Oh, you are men of stones.
> Had I your tongues and eyes, I'd use them so
> That heaven's vault should crack. She's gone for ever.
> I know when one is dead and when one lives.
> She's dead as earth. Lend me a looking glass.
> If that her breath will mist or stain the stone,
> Why, then she lives. (5.3.258–64)

Tolstoy's summary is eight words longer than the original: "Lear enters with the dead Cordelia in his arms, notwithstanding the fact that he is past eighty and sick. And Lear's horrible delirium begins again, which makes one ashamed, like an unsuccessful joke. Lear demands that everybody howl, and sometimes thinks Cordelia is dead, sometimes that she is alive. 'Had I,' he says, 'your tongues and eyes, I would use them so that the heavens would crack'" (Tolstoy, *PSS*, 35:235).

This is not the bloodless summary students read in *CliffsNotes*, but one literary genius doing a demolition job on another. The central technique here is a version of the defamiliarization for which Tolstoy is famous. Morphologically, "howl!" is an imperative, but Lear's words do not demand or even implore empathy so much as they enunciate the horror of the universe. Tolstoy literalizes them, just as he adds "he says" in the middle of a deeply moving quotation, using the commas as much as the words to interrupt the reader's response. He does the same thing with the storm scene:

> Blow, winds, and crack your cheeks! rage! blow!
> You cataracts and hurricanoes, spout
> Till you have drenched our steeples, drowned the cocks!
> You sulph'rous and thought-executing fires,
> Vaunt-couriers of oak-cleaving thunderbolts,
> singe my white head! (3.2.1–6)

Tolstoy's narration of this speech is as narrative as Shakespeare's presentation is dramatic: "Lear walks across the heath [*po stepi*] and says words which are supposed to express his despair: he wants the winds to blow in such a way that their ('the winds') cheeks would burst, the rain to pour over everything and the lightning to singe his gray hair, the thunder to crush the earth and destroy all the seeds that make an ungrateful person" (Tolstoy, *PSS*, 35:226).

The humor again resides in large part in Tolstoy's literalism. He reports Lear's raging as if Lear were conveying information: the idea that one must specify exactly whose cheeks should burst projects the same naïveté as the idea of summarizing such a speech by saying, "he . . ." And Tolstoy has already covered himself against the kind of literary analysis I am making by saying that these are words which are supposed to express Lear's despair. Unlike *CliffsNotes*, this kind of summary presupposes its reader's acquaintance with the original. It is a text about a text, not about an unfortunate king.

Tolstoy, as it happens, denied that Shakespeare was a major playwright and considered his renown to be the kind of rampant and then inertial suggestion to which humanity has always been subject (and still is). He cites the Children's Crusades, those of grownups too, the witch hunts, the belief in the effectiveness of torture to determine the truth, the pursuit of the elixir of life, the philosopher's stone, and the seventeenth-century tulip mania as other examples (Tolstoy, *PSS*, 35:260).

Tolstoy loved to shock, and some of his distaste for *King Lear* reflects this need to be noticed and some reflects his distrust of lyricism and secularism, both of which were dear to Shakespeare. He explains the ongoing excitement with the play as the inertia of popular delusions:

> In Roman times it was already perceived that books have destinies of their own and often very strange ones: failure, notwithstanding their high worth and vast, undeserved success, notwithstanding their insignificance. And the pronouncement was made *pro capite lectoris habent sua fata libelli*, that is, the fate of books depends on reader reception. Such was the correspondence of the works of Shakespeare to the world outlook of the people among whom that renown arose. The renown was supported, and is to this day, because the works of Shakespeare continue to answer the world-outlook of the people who support that renown.
>
> (Tolstoy, *PSS*, 35:262)

The renown of *King Lear*, as we know, did not protect its plot. Through most of the eighteenth century, audiences saw only Nahum Tate's improved version, which enabled the old king to survive and for Cordelia to marry Edgar. The Romantics finally returned Shakespeare's original plot to the stage.

Tolstoy did not carry these doctrines of reader response to the point where the text does not matter. In fact, he compared those doctrines so devoid of aesthetic feeling as to praise Shakespeare with blind men trying to sort out diamonds from heaps of pebbles, who would conclude "that all stones are precious, especially the smoothest." On the broadest level, Tolstoy rejected Shakespeare because his style was Elizabethan and because he was unreligious; long since, in *What Is Art?*, he had proclaimed that art should infect the audience with the highest religious ideas of its time. But when he singles out *King Lear* to attack, he does so on the basis of plot.

Let us look for a moment at another key moment in the plot of *King Lear*. When Lear wakes up after his madness, he sees Cordelia and says,

> You do me wrong to take me out o' the grave.
> Thou art a soul in bliss; but I am bound
> Upon a wheel of fire, that mine own tears
> Do scald like molten lead.
> ...
> You are a spirit, I know. Where did you die?
> ...
> Do not laugh at me;
> For (as I am a man) I think this lady
> To be my child Cordelia.
> ...
> Be your tears wet? Yes, faith.   (4.7.44–47, 48, 67–69, 70)

This is plainly a recognition scene. Lear believes he and Cordelia are both dead, himself in torment and Cordelia in heaven. His own death would be understandable. He is old, five years older than Tolstoy when the latter wrote about the play, and he has been through rages and wanderings more harrowing than those which killed Tolstoy a few years later. But there is a glitch in the causal system: Lear has exiled Cordelia to be queen of France; he did not order her execution, and nobody has lied to him about her death. This speech belongs in another kind of play. In this other kind of play, a ruler is or feels that he is responsible for the death of a good and beautiful woman who has nevertheless survived, usually because people lied to him. This speech comes from the recognition scene of such a play. If many chronologies are right, Shakespeare had recently written one such scene, in *All's Well That Ends Well* (5.3.304f). When Helena appears, the King expresses the astonishment Bertram and the others feel: "Is there no exorcist / beguiles the truer office of mine eyes? / Is't real that I see?" (5.3.340–42). He soon wrote another about Pericles, who thinks his wife has sickened and died bearing his child and been buried at sea:

> CERIMON: This is your wife.
> PERICLES: Reverend appearer, no;
>   I threw her overboard with these very arms.
> . . .
> CERIMON: Early one morning this lady was
>   Thrown upon this shore. I oped the coffin,
>   Found these rich jewels, recovered her . . .
> . . .
> THAISA: O my Lord, are you not Pericles? Like him you spake,
>   Like him you are. Did you not name a tempest,
>   A birth, and death?
> PERICLES: The voice of dead Thaisa!
>
> (*Pericles, Prince of Tyre*, 5.3.19–21, 25–27, 35–39)

This recognition scene is generated not by a lie, but by an error about a death at sea, as in *A Comedy of Errors* and *Twelfth Night*.

In *Cymbeline*, as we have seen, a king of Britain, one as mythical as Lear, thinks Imogen has been killed as punishment for adultery and then learns she was innocent. When he sees her alive, he says, "If this be so, the gods do mean to strike me to death with mortal joy. . . . The tune of Imogen!" (5.5.270–76).

And in *The Winter's Tale*, King Leontes has learned that the orders he gave for Hermione's death were unwarranted. She has survived and is placed in a niche like a statue. The king addresses it:

> LEONTES: Her natural posture!
>   Chide me, dear stone, that I may say indeed
>   Thou art Hermione.
> . . .

LEONTES: Give me that hand of yours to kiss.

PAULINA: O patience!
    The statue is but newly fixed; the color's
    not dry.

. . .

LEONTES: Oh, she's warm!   (5.3.29–31, 55–58, 135)

These four recognition scenes all start with the visual and are clinched by the auditory or tactile. When Lear says, "Be your tears wet," or at the end of the play when he says, "Her voice was ever soft and low, a most excellent thing in woman," Shakespeare is plainly pursuing a practice he would exploit in his romances and probably already had used in *All's Well That Ends Well*. I know that Shakespeare is reported never to have blotted a line he wrote, but I still would suggest that these lines survive in *King Lear* from an early draft, in which Cordelia survives and comforts Lear in his royal old age. Shakespeare inherited this ending from *The True Chronicle History of King Leir*; Tate preferred it, and Tolstoy praised the earlier play as far superior to Lear.

Shakespeare, I would argue, did due diligence and tried his hand at the plot he inherited. He wrote the culmination of all his recognition scenes, but then decided that he wasn't ready for his late romances. He had a huge task: first, he replaced the execution order with banishment, though he left the rage that could have motivated either order in a lesser king. But then he ran out of negative capability and couldn't bear to put aside the most beautiful thing he'd ever made and use it in a lesser play. This leaves us with the only recognition scene in Shakespeare that does not correct a lie or a maritime error.

In a letter written long before his article, Tolstoy had once said King Lear ought to be a usurper. That way he would not be "a man more sinned against than sinning." Tolstoy was willing to accept the suffering in Greek drama because it had religious meaning. William Empson once commented on Hamlet's phrase about knowing a hawk from a handsaw, being sane. A German commentator had corrected this distinction to that between a hawk and a hansel, or male goose. Empson said that this commentator had restored an earlier version of Hamlet's line. Hamlet, being Hamlet, had thought of knowing a hawk from a hansel and then gone one better, one weirder, closer to a modernist simile. The commentator, as Empson put it, was "unwriting Shakespeare." Tolstoy and Tate, I suggest, were both unwriting *King Lear*. They had both felt the presence of an older plot. Shakespeare had too. He had read the older play and, some think, acted in it. If he could have read Tolstoy's and Tate's improvements, he would have said, "Been there, tried that, wrote *King Lear* instead."

PART III

THE PLOT OF *CRIME AND PUNISHMENT* DRAWS RHETORICAL AND MORAL POWER FROM THE NATURE OF NOVEL PLOTS AND FROM THE EUROPEAN AND RUSSIAN TRADITION DOSTOEVSKY INHERITED AND DEVELOPED

14

European Novelists Elaborated or Assembled Incidents into Plots Long Before Critics Recognized the Sophistication of the New Genre in Plotting Such Subgenres as the Letter Novel and the Detective Novel

Novels, like epics, histories, and biographies, differ from dramas in two central ways: they are longer and they are narrative. We have studied the ways Shakespeare made the classical, medieval, and Renaissance plots that he inherited longer by obsessively returning to the formulas of the parallel plot and the play-within-a-play, where one character shapes the interactions of others. This practice keeps the plot fractal, recapitulating in the part the dramatically enacted nature of the whole. The novel on the other hand, as it evolved out of existing forms, acquired its defining length primarily by narrative means, occasionally using characters who manipulate others into their own dramas, but more often relying on the narrative device of a story within or about a story. The plot of each genre gets longer along the axis of its literary identity.

E. M. Forster defined a novel as a piece of prose fiction more than fifty thousand words long. How do novels get to be long? Y. K. Shcheglov and A. K. Zholkovsky typify one type of answer when they describe the way an author expands a "theme" such as "a wolf in sheep's clothing" into the kind of plot summary Aarne or Polti might list: "Someone, while feigning protection or friendship, prepares to murder his protégé," and then goes on to expand this summary into a text. A more historical approach describes how the novel evolved out of collections of anecdotes, novellas, letters, or other small literary genres. Reversing these two processes, readers can either summarize a large work down to its generating incident or analyze a large work into its component incidents.

This cast of mind that generates a text out of a single incident or summarizes it back into one incident shares one perception with that other cast of mind which assembles a text out of many incidents or analyzes it back into its component parts: both show both sides of the old paradox of the one and the many—plots are both wholes and complexities. Each of these approaches has its uses. Generative grammarians, alchemists, and Gestalt psychologists have the first cast of mind, and structural linguists, Greek atomists, and nineteenth-century positivists the second. Both casts of mind seek to describe the beautiful order in the world or in a text.

Some of the finest literary minds have a third approach: texts, like the world, aren't orderly—they're messy. Common sense denies that *Tristram Shandy* can have a beginning, a middle, and an end because Sterne would almost certainly have added to it had he lived longer. *Anna Karenina* cannot have a preconceived plot; near the end, Vronsky goes off to a war that did not exist when the first chapters were published. But common sense can be dangerous. We shall see things in *Crime and Punishment* that were not messy at all, but looked messy to good readers. Homer nods, and so does Dostoevsky; personal, historical, and other events certainly influence texts. But those concerns make our job too easy. A great book is a fearsome thing, and always tempts a reader to talk about something else. I need to know all I can about an author's health, psyche, readings, interaction with society, and so forth, but my profession demands that I seek order in the text, knowing that I may fail, just as doctors seek to prolong lives knowing their patients are mortal.

The orderly and reproducible arrangement of parts to form a whole is a structure. The orderly and reproducible transformation of one whole to form another can be an algorithm. The structural approach treats certain relationships very well; others respond better to an algorithmic approach. The figure below, for example, can be described structurally as a square with rectangular inflections at its corners, oriented verti-cally at the upper-right and lower-left corners and horizontally at the other two corners, with four smaller rectangles, oppositely oriented, arrayed on the same axes inside the indented corners.

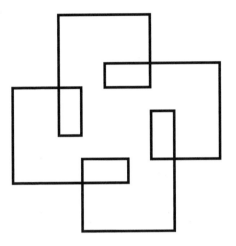

With proper measurements added, this spatial description would en-able a careful reader to reproduce this drawing. But an algorithm oper-ating in time, not space, would permit the reproduction of the drawing far more easily: from a starting point, draw a line one unit long; turn 90 degrees to the left and draw a line two units long; turn left again and draw a line three units long, then four, then five; start over.

A literary text can look messy but have an order that is not structural but algorithmic.

According to most definitions of what a novel is, people have been writing novels in the West for only a few centuries, as opposed to plays, which have been around for millennia. Up to Dostoevsky's own time, novels tended to be regarded as less deserving of serious attention than most of the older genres. James Boswell reports that in 1781 when Miss Monckton told Samuel Johnson that Sterne had affected her with his pa-thos, he answered, "That is because, dearest, you're a dunce." His apol-ogy is one of the best in our language—"If I had thought so, I certainly should not have said it"—but it withdraws his opinion not of novels, but of the woman; women get upset more easily than novels.

Until the nineteenth century, critics and novelists often talked about novelistic plots as a prose variant of epic plots. In part, this practice simply followed Aristotle, who happened, for all his learning, not to have read any novels, but who wrote briefly and well about epics. Fielding set *Tom Jones* in the parallel antique tradition of the mock epic, which led him to highly sophisticated discourse about the use of time in fiction. We have mentioned the Hellenistic critics' attention to the collision between time in the fabula and time in the siuzhet when Homer begins in medias res. University courses in epic still include novels and vice versa, and the adjective "epic" is still a term of high praise in book reviewery. But Bakhtin has persuaded much of the literary community that the novel is really the opposite of the epic, that the epic at its purest valorizes the language, the thinking, and the lifestyle of the old establishment, saying, "There were giants on the earth in those days, and also after that," whereas a novel is inherently subversive and leaves the current and the past state of things open to ongoing question.

Despite Bakhtin's sense that novels function differently in society from epics, their plots draw directly and indirectly from a multitude of epic techniques. Folk narrative traditions often start with a long list of heroes, each with his own adventure or two. Audiences would demand one more story about their favorite hero, so singers would tell a minor hero's story about a more popular hero. Gradually, these augmented collections of stories would sometimes find causal connections, as in the *Iliad*, or chronological connections, as in the *Odyssey*. Novels recapitulated this process that generated epic. Collections of individual plots had existed for centuries. Some drive for coherence would lead these plots into a text that united them in just one important way. They might be united by having a single narrator (like *The Arabian Nights*), or by being told at a single place or time (like *The Decameron*), or having a single hero (like the picaresque tales).

These proto-novels also emerge from a dozen other genres. Scholars in the 1970s and 1980s made much of the fact that narration in histories and narration in novels follow many of the same patterns, but novelists had noticed this long before, as can be seen from the number of early novels entitled "The True History of . . . ," or in the nineteenth and twentieth centuries, "The Chronicle of. . . ." Here, the word "true" designates the fictional nature of the text. In the sixteenth and seventeenth centuries, novelists invented the modern novelistic plot, in imitation of memoirs, biographies, and collections of letters, all ancient nonfictional genres that flourished anew in the Baroque period, but also in imitation of Greek romance, Roman prose fiction, and medieval romance (in prose and poetry), as well as the medieval Latin, Greek, and Arabic short story and novella collections. In the web of intellectual history, such multiple influences often operate through nodal figures who sum up a huge body of experience and become the source for all but the esoterically learned in later generations. Don Quixote serves this function in the history of the European novelistic plot.

For his central plot, Cervantes sets out to mock the improbabilities in the causal systems of chivalric romance, both the intervention of supernatural forces and the implausible motivation of the knights; but for the arrangement of the embedded episodes he draws from epic and the picaresque tradition of epics, whose most visible connection is chronological: "And then another incident occurred." As in *The Arabian Nights*, the central relation among these many plot incidents is not causal and only occasionally one of parallelism or contrast, but rather a relation of narrative containment. In other genres, a group of narrators meet on a pilgrimage, in a bivouac, in flight from a plague. Don Quixote interacts with a string of characters he encounters, but he also listens to their narrations, which usually have little or no causal connection with his own adventures. Cervantes almost footnotes his debt to historians, to memoirists, and to Arabs by placing most of the account of the Don in the memoir written by the fictional Arabic historian, Cide Hamete Benengeli. All this reflects the zaniness of the plot containment in *The Arabian Nights*, as the Don even encounters people who have read about him.

This recycling of the Latin and Arabic plot connections has much to do with the Spanish invention of the picaresque novel, whose hero, like Petronius's, lacks most of the endearing virtues but enlists our involvement because he is kept before us all the time. If we met such a picaro in real life, we would either work hard to avoid him or else exploit him as a literary artifact of our own, in the genre of dinner-table conversation. The grinding paradox of *Crime and Punishment*—that we care about the well-being of a calculating, self-absorbed hatchet-murderer—rests in part on the picaresque way the narration obsessively focuses our attention on him as he rushes from crisis to crisis.

In the seventeenth and eighteenth centuries, many of Cervantes's most famous successors mimicked not histories but collections of letters, partly because collections of real letters and manuals for letter-writing were popular, but also because the classical collections of letters—such as Cicero's, or the fictional *Heroides* of Ovid—offered something rare in Latin fiction: plotting based on psychological causality. In the eighteenth and early nineteenth centuries, Russia produced popular and interesting epistolary novels, but none as important as those of Samuel Richardson, Jean-Jacques Rousseau, Johann Wolfgang von Goethe, or Pierre Choderlos de Laclos. The beginnings of the letter novel are obscured by the difficulty of distinguishing a novel from a collection of real letters. Natascha Wurzbach cites a rule of thumb that works most of the time: if a book of letters contains unclear references and discontinuities and needs a commentary, it is real; if it makes sense, it's fiction.

A century ago, readers tended to follow Melchior de Vogüé's 1881 doctrine that Dostoevsky was a wild man, remote from Western culture and unable to control himself. Since then, the study of his notebooks, his reading list, and his novels themselves has shown that he crafted them diligently, self-consciously, and with constant attention to Western authors and intellectuals. He borrowed plots and plotting techniques from his omnivorous reading. But if public taste and fashion strongly favored or neglected some literary figure or practice, Dostoevsky would often do the reverse. In 1846, when he decided to begin his creative career with a novel in letters, serious authors had abandoned the form a generation earlier.

Sheer perversity explains this decision most easily. Dostoevsky liked to shock and needed public attention. But more importantly, letter novels offered resources that matched Dostoevsky's literary needs. Letter novels appeal to certain kinds of authors. We have noticed that incidents in the fabula are causally related to one another in two ways, one inside the characters' heads and one outside. An action novel or a political novel may largely ignore the first way; a novel of ideas or a social novel may operate either way; and a psychological novel by definition must pay major attention to drives, goals, motives, reactions, and other internal causations.

Early novelists had to invent ways to narrate a character's thoughts and feelings. First-person narration was one method, but presented technical difficulties: how does the narrator know things he or she does not see or hear, including the thoughts or feelings of other characters? Omniscient narration presented other problems: how does one gracefully withhold information from the reader, etc.? In the seventeenth and eighteenth centuries, the great letter novels evolved a *motivirovka* to enter the minds of two or more characters, to perceive the same sequences of incidents in different ways, and to triangulate a given incident through two or more sets of responses, so that narration interacts very closely with plot.

Dostoevsky's *Poor Folk* exploits this obsolete and sometime clumsy technique. In the chapters that follow, we will find elements in this novel that throw light on the plot of *Crime and Punishment*. The plotting in Dostoevsky's fiction evolved much as plotting did in the history of the Russian novel, which in turn recapitulates the history of the European novel.

15

Dostoevsky Shaped and Was Shaped by the Russian Version of the Nineteenth-Century Novel

For all the depth of his debt to European novelists, Dostoevsky was standing on the shoulders of Nikolai Karamzin (1766–1826), Alexander Pushkin (1799–1837), Mikhail Lermontov (1814–1841), and Nikolai Gogol (1809–1852), the giants who founded nineteenth-century prose fiction in Russia. The first and the last of these authors were both called "the Russian Sterne," and Dostoevsky called the last two his "demons." Culturally, eighteenth- and nineteenth-century Russia resolutely faced West; even its use of the literature and art of its Asian empire emulated European Orientalism. In the non-literary world, architects, engineers, admirals, musicians, cooks, and religious cultists moved between the Russian Empire and the West with no break in their careers; yet in the history of the novel, where the Russian Empire arguably made its greatest contribution to world culture, the plot assumed a different role.

It has been argued that Sterne's mockery of eighteenth-century novels was so devastating that serious authors stopped writing them, driving Walter Scott and the Gothic novelists in England to invent a new kind of novel, which flourished throughout the nineteenth century. This chapter will argue that the nineteenth-century Russian novel escaped that devastation and offered Dostoevsky and other Russians an eighteenth-century energy, especially in Sterne's specialty, narrative technique.

Charles Dickens, William Makepeace Thackeray, and many others construct a narrator who sometimes becomes a friend and almost a co-conspirator of the reader. One of Thackeray's narrators, Pendennis, even becomes a character in a later novel. This tight link between narration and character gives verisimilitude to the European novel. In the same years, Tolstoy, Dostoevsky, and many other Russians were moving in a different direction, elaborating a link between narration and plot.

Melchior de Vogüé, the French diplomat, journalist, and gossip, called Dostoevsky a "true Scythian," a non-European, but the split between Russian and European prose fiction owes no more to Dostoevsky's forced stay in Omsk than to Tolstoy's education in Eastern culture at Kazan, or to the travels of Pushkin, Lermontov, Leskov, Ivan Goncharov, Vladimir Korolenko, Anton Chekhov, or others through Russia's vast empire in Asia. Rather, it reflects Russia's status, which Alexis de Tocqueville compared to America's, as one of Europe's cultural colonies, where partial outsiders found riches in the hegemonic culture to which proximity, familiarity, or the pressures of fashion blinded those at the center. No culture can either be fully independent or use its own resources fully. When a hegemonic artistic tradition reaches a crossroads, its subcultures sometimes realize possibilities excluded by the course the dominant culture takes.

In the first Western study of the Russian novel, de Vogüé refers to "the intellectual discipline, the clarity, the precision, virtues which are so rare among the prose writers of Russia" (*The Russian Novel*, 197). A generation later, Henry James praised the power and richness of Russian novels, but his famous letter to Hugh Walpole called them "fluid puddings" (*Letters*, 4:619), and he complained to Mrs. Humphrey Ward about Tolstoy's "promiscuous shifting of viewpoint and center" (112), perhaps reflecting de Vogüé's description of what he felt on reading Dostoevsky: "The shiver that seizes us on encountering some of his characters makes one wonder whether one is in the presence of genius, but one quickly remembers that genius in letters does not exist without two higher gifts, measure and universality" (*The Russian Novel*, 267).

James's prefaces contain the first subtle exposition of the novelistic techniques that evolved in the West in the nineteenth century, and his novels may be the least provincial ever written. Yet, somehow, he failed to realize that the rules for narrative technique, "viewpoint and center," that he presented were not universal aspects of the psychology of art but the conventions of a particular time and place.

The Russian interdependence between plotting and narration constituted a very different, but no less demanding, kind of technical mastery than that developed by Scott, Dickens, Thackeray, and James. Western critics sometimes distinguish novels that tell readers what happens from novels that show them what happens; the Russian novelistic techniques let Tolstoy, Dostoevsky, and others go beyond both of these Western practices and manipulate readers into experiencing for themselves what the characters in the novel are feeling and arguing. The Russians adopted this manipulative goal from Rousseau, Sterne, and other Sentimental novelists of the eighteenth century.

Written in the generation before Dostoevsky, Lermontov's novel *A Hero of Our Time* (1840) links plot with narration in a particularly vivid way. It is almost an encyclopedia of alternative causal connections between incidents. Narratively, the voices, experiences, and actions of the characters reach the reader through the accounts of the old soldier Maksim Maksimich or the Byronic aristocrat Pechorin, which are filtered through the voice of an "editor," who sometimes selects the materials from "a thick notebook" and always edits at least the names to protect the "real" people the novel imagines. And from the 1841 edition on, a preface interposes the outermost voice of an authorial figure who knows that all the others are fictional. Such narrative layering was commonplace in Russia and the West in the 1830s, but Lermontov's different figures inhabit very different worlds, knowing about different incidents and, more importantly, seeing totally different causal mechanisms as organizing these incidents.

In most novels, as we have said, the dominant relationship among the incidents in the fabula is cause and effect, or its psychological reflex, motivation, but *A Hero of Our Time* goes beyond this practical use of causality and becomes a philosophical dialogue among the characters and the narrators on the nature of causality. On the first page of the novel, the "editor" introduces the topic with a question that naively applies a certain causal system: "How is it that four oxen can haul your loaded carriage like a lark, and six of the creatures can scarcely budge my empty one with the help of these Ossetians?" This editor's world operates by the laws of physics or, when he predicts a fine morrow, by appearances. On the other hand, Maksim Maksimich operates in a world of hidden causes, explaining how the Ossetian greed for extra business makes them impede their own oxen, or how the steam rising from a distant mountain presages a blizzard. Though he is the central figure of the novel, in this first story Pechorin is only a minor narrator, but near the end of this story, he introduces a Byronic system of motivation into a story where other characters have motives out of a Walter Scott novel: "Listen, Maksim Maksimich . . . I have an unhappy character: whether my upbringing made me so, or God made me so, I don't know; I know only that if I am the cause of unhappiness to others, I am no less unhappy." Maksim Maksimich is as naive about such Byronism as the "editor" is about the Caucasus:

> "Did the French bring boredom into fashion?"
> —"No, the English.—
> "Aha, that's it. . . . Of course, they always were outrageous drunkards." (214)

Maksim Maksimich introduces not only ethnic, economic, atmospheric, and alcoholic determinism into the causal system; a dozen pages later he also uses social class to explain behavior: "What are we uneducated oldsters doing, chasing after you? . . . You're young society folk, proud; as long as you're here under the Cherkassian bullets, you're O.K. . . . But if you meet us afterwards you're ashamed to offer your hand to one of us" (228).

Maksim Maksimich's causes relate incidents to one another in the realistic tradition, contrasting not only with the physical causality the editor espouses, but also with the romantic kinds of causes Pechorin invokes: "These eyes, it seemed, were endowed with some magnetic power" (235); "the bumps on his skull . . . would have astonished a phrenologist with the strange mix of conflicting drives" (248); "We're reading one another in the heart" (249), etc.

For Dostoevsky, more important than such phrases are four especially Russian features of causation in Pechorin's accounts: coincidence, including all of Pechorin's accidental eavesdropping; the sovereign power of the will, as when Pechorin draws a group of listeners away from other entertaining interlocutors, or when he makes his opponent miss his shot in their duel; the gratuitous actions motivated not by anything external but by the nature of the character, such as that which makes Pechorin wonder "why I did not want to set out on that path fate had opened to me where quiet joys and heartfelt calm awaited me? . . . No, I should never have adapted to that destiny" (312); and finally, fate, which he discusses throughout, but most especially in the final story of the novel.

This complex of Pechorinesque causations never exists alone, because his narrative voice never exists alone. At the end of the novel, Maksim Maksimich initially responds to Pechorin's account of an experiment in Russian roulette that appeared to confirm predestination: "Yes, sir. It's a rather tricky matter! . . . Still, these Asiatic triggers often misfire, if they're badly oiled." The novel seems to have two fabulas, one organizing events according to the rules of practical life and another according to the more exciting rules of Pechorin's world. Lermontov gives Pechorin the last word about fatalism, but it is a strikingly indecisive comment on the entire panoply of causal systems that this novel explores in its plot and narration: "[Maksim Maksimich] in general dislikes metaphysical debates."

Nikolai Karamzin had carried the eighteenth-century Sentimental tradition from the West into Russian nineteenth-century prose much as Lermontov later popularized Romanticism. In Karamzin's "My Confession" (1802), the narrator prides himself on his lack of honor, sanity, and social value, carrying Rousseau's willful taboo-breaking and gratuitous actions to a level of insulting self-consciousness that sounds less like Rousseau's *Confessions* than like Dostoevsky's *Notes from Underground*, though Dostoevsky was drawing on both. Karamzin's most famous short story, "Poor Liza" (1792), appealed to the sentiment that expresses itself through tears, though the Sentimentalist aesthetic also valorizes the emotions that produce laughter, social action, and many other responses. Liza is a young flower-seller on the Moscow streets who is seduced and abandoned by the wealthy Erast. She dies pathetically.

In his role of follower, competitor, and successor to Karamzin as the central figure on the Russian literary scene, Pushkin seems at first to belong to the Western nineteenth-century novelistic tradition, as Ivan Turgenev did in his major novels and as did many lesser novelists in Pushkin's generation, such as Osip Senkovsky, Nikolai Polevoy, Alexander Bestuzhev-Marlinsky, Faddei Bulgarin, Anton Pogorelsky, Ivan Lazhechnikov, Alexander Veltman, or Mikhail Zagoskin. Certainly Pushkin loved the fashionable and was drenched in Western literature; his *Captain's Daughter* (1836) draws its setting and much of its plot from Walter Scott's *Waverley* (1814). Yet the works of Pushkin that most influenced later Russian novels were not conventional novels at all. One was *Eugene Onegin* (1833), a novel in verse, and the other was *The Belkin Tales* (1830), which are usually treated as a group of separate stories, like Karamzin's, not as a proto-novelistic experiment. The plotting in *Onegin* follows the standard pattern René Girard ascribes to European novels: desire is imitative and unreciprocated. Onegin rejects Tatiana's love until he sees her loved, then she rejects him when he offers himself to her. But in both of these works, the narrator stands back and reflects upon the incidents in ways that seem sometimes naive and sometimes remarkably sophisticated. The narrator of *Eugene Onegin* cries out "Alas!" like a Sentimental novelist and digresses like Fielding or Sterne, although he also enters with the reader into conspiratorial judgment of his hero in the manner of Scott or later, Dickens and Thackeray. Pushkin may draw his plots from contemporary Europe, but his narrative technique in *Onegin* retains much of Sterne's, Fielding's, or Voltaire's eighteenth-century flexibility and playfulness, with a "preface" at the end of chapter 7 and a siuzhet containing much detail about the life and opinions of the narrator that plays no part at all in the lives of the characters.

The Belkin Tales fall midway through the evolution of the most ambitious Russian prose in the 1820s and 1830s as it recapitulated the long and intricate history of the proto-novel in Europe, moving from collections of individual tales, like Karamzin's and the *Gesta Romanorum* (c. 1300), to tales linked by a narrative situation like Bestuzhev-Marlinsky's *Evenings on the Bivouac* (1823) and Boccaccio's *Decameron* (1360s), through tales linked by a single narrator like Pushkin's Belkin and Thomas Malory's narrator in *Le Morte d'Arthur* (1485), to tales linked by a single hero, like *Don Quixote* (1605) and Lermontov's *A Hero of our Time* (1840), which is fractal, a collection of incidents worked into stories and stories incorporated into a novel. Such evolution never occurs neatly; early techniques often attract late writers more than prescient recent works of isolated geniuses, but the Russians were able to do in decades what took centuries in the West precisely because in addition to the classical sources in epic and romance from Petronius, Apuleius, and others which shaped the Western novel, the Russians had an existing novelistic tradition developed by Fyodor Emin, Mikhail Chulkov, and others in the eighteenth century and, far more important, the rich novelistic tradition of the West to draw on.

Pushkin's Belkin breaks Henry James's cardinal rule for a narrator. James's narrators may be wise or foolish, even insane or fanatic, but they must be consistently whatever they are, so that "the interest created, and the expression of that interest, are things kept, as to kind, genuine and true to themselves" (*The Art of the Novel*, 97). Moreover, narrators who can see into a character's mind at one moment must not learn what that character is thinking from his countenance at another moment (16). Belkin begins telling "The Blizzard" with full insight into the mind of the heroine and suddenly switches to the narration of her actions entirely from outside. Pushkin breaks James's rules here not through ignorance or inattention, but simply because other literary needs precluded obedience to such rules. The effectiveness of the siuzhet demands that the reader share the heroine's bookish but wholehearted love and also her surprise at the ending of the story. Consistency would have cost him one or the other of these effects, and Pushkin therefore turned to the eighteenth-century tradition of more flexible narrators.

Pushkin liked and admired Karamzin, but disdained his Sentimentalism. He mischievously took the plot of "Poor Liza" and offered an alternative ending in Belkin's tale "The Station Agent." The poor agent in a remote station for changing stagecoach horses dies of despondency when a rich and dashing seducer carries off his daughter to a ruin explored in an earlier generation by Richardson and many others. But to mourn him, the daughter returns grandly in a coach and four. In defiance of the Sentimental plot formula, she is the victor and has seduced her victim into the ultimate comeuppance for the promiscuous: marriage. Belkin offers no information about what goes on in the psyche of either combatant during this battle of the sexes.

The hero of Dostoevsky's first novel, *Poor Folk* (1846), reads this story and sorrows for the old station agent, as Karamzin would have wanted. He also resembles the agent, losing the object of his affection to a rich seducer who carries her away in a coach. But Dostoevsky shows us every step in her subjection of this suitor, from her revulsion after the seducer's earlier mistreatment of her, through her heartbroken abandonment of the poor clerk who longs to starve with her, to the moment she reduces the seducer to buying her things he cannot afford, and the true comeuppance, marriage. Dostoevsky has used the letter form to turn the plot of two of the greatest Russian short stories into that of a psychological novel that dares to compete with Pushkin and Karamzin.

The reasons Dostoevsky could draw on eighteenth-century techniques that Dickens, Gustave Flaubert, and others rejected can be summed up in two words: Nikolai Gogol. Like Karamzin, as we have said, Gogol has been called the Russian Sterne. While the Western Europeans drew a new kind of novel from the tradition of Scott and the Gothic novelists because Sterne had carried so many eighteenth-century novelistic techniques to the point of absurdity, the Russians also drew heavily on the sensationalism of E. T. A. Hoffmann and Gothic novels coupled with the sharp social, moral, and psychological judgment of Scott's novels. But they never turned away from Sterne. Gogol's first novel, *Taras Bulba* (1835), owes much to Scott; yet Gogol also enabled the Russians to go on developing the techniques of the eighteenth-century Western novels they had been reading in translation and in the original for generations. A short story that appeared almost simultaneously with *A Hero of Our Time* gives the clearest illustration of Gogol's departure from the Western European tradition later canonized in Henry James's prefaces.

"The Tale of How Ivan Ivanovich Quarreled with Ivan Nikiforovich" (1835) seems at first to be an almost plotless story of provincial pettiness, anger, and stupidity; two old friends quarrel over an insignificant request and go through their whole lives unreconciled. In the first sentences of the story, the narrator seems to be equally involved in matters of limited significance: "Ivan Ivanovich has a glorious jacket! The most excellent! And what soft fleece! Whew, go to, what wool! I'll wager Lord knows that you can't find anybody's like it!" (Gogol, *PSS*, 2:223)

These words give little information about Ivan Ivanovich but a great deal about the narrator. He is still close enough to infancy to love fuzz, to end every phrase with an exclamation point, and to bubble over with enthusiasm at matters that most of us might at most consider nice. Three pages later, this narrator remains enthusiastic and naive, but already has acquired enough control of himself and the world to enter into sociological, statistical, and perhaps biological disputation:

> It has been spread around that Ivan Nikiforovich was born with a tail at his back. But this canard is so absurd and at the same time stupid and indecent that I judge it unnecessary to refute it before enlightened readers, who are aware without the slightest doubt, that only witches, and even very few of them have tails at their backs; and they, moreover, belong for the most part to the female sex rather than the male. (2:226)

Whatever our views on the statistics of caudal preponderance, we all can recognize a much more mature voice than that of the narrator at the beginning of the story. When he appears again twenty pages later, this narrator has developed the voice of a jaded traveler with a clear and ironic sense of the Russian bureaucracy: "The trial then moved with that uncommon speed for which our judiciary is so widely renowned. They annotated papers, excerpted them, numbered them, bound them, and receipted them all on one and the same day, and placed it all in a cabinet where it lay, lay, lay a year another, a third" (2:263). And a few pages later, the narrator has even acquired literary self-consciousness: "No, I cannot! . . . Give me another pen! My pen is faded, deadened, with too thin a stroke for this picture!" (2:271). Finally, on the last two pages of the story, a conscientious, self-important, and tired old man displays no trace of enthusiasm: "At that time, the weather exercised a strong effect on me: I grew bored when it was boring. . . . I sighed still more deeply and hurried to make my adieus because I was traveling on a quite important matter, and got into my carriage. . . . It's boring on this earth, gentlemen!" (2:276)

This final exclamation point has nothing in common with those at the beginning of the story. These last words almost coincide with Winston Churchill's confession of boredom to his last private secretary, Anthony Montague Browne, while dying in his tenth decade. Henry James would call this changing narrator loose and baggy, a danger to the reliability that rests on the integrity of the figure through whom the reader must apprehend everything in the text. And yet Gogol orders these changes tightly. His narrator has rather more of a career than any other character in the story. Readers see the growing decrepitude and pointlessness of the officials, the provincial town and the two Ivans, and, without noticing it, they also experience the aging of the narrator and his unsuccessful struggle against the pointlessness of his existence. By breaking the narrative rules of the West and giving his narrator a plot of his own, Gogol implicates the reader in the aging process.

16

In Reinventing the Psychological Plot, Dostoevsky Challenged the Current Literary Leaders

Dostoevsky's hero in *Poor Folk* is a poor, abused copy clerk in the vast Xerox-less Russian bureaucracy, as is the hero of Gogol's most famous short story, "The Overcoat" (1842). The hero of *Poor Folk* reads this story, as he does "The Station Agent," and reacts with the same unsophisticated sorrow. This sorrow carries Dostoevsky into direct competition with Gogol. The plot of all of Gogol's greatest works is very simple: paradise lost. Usually, it is fairy-gifts, a nonexistent paradise: the estate of the hero of *Dead Souls*, or the greatness of the Inspector General. In "The Overcoat," the paradise is, for a moment, really there. The poor clerk shivers and starves himself until he can buy an overcoat, and rejoices in it; when it is stolen, he dies. We have learned about his psyche primarily from what happens to him and what he does. Dostoevsky's poor clerk also loses the object of his longing, that for which he has starved and sacrificed, but this is a human being, not a piece of cloth. And his hero has poured out a soul in his letters. Dostoevsky has challenged the two greatest writers of the previous generation by taking the plots of two of their greatest stories and giving their heroes psyches.

By the time he wrote *Crime and Punishment*, Dostoevsky had long since turned, as the European novel had two generations earlier, from the letter novel to the mature psychological novel. After a decade in prison camp and exile, Dostoevsky returned to a St. Petersburg where *Dead Souls* and *Eugene Onegin* were about to relinquish center stage to a new, radical, idealistic, and, in fact, ideological novel, Chernyshevsky's *What Is to Be Done?* (1863). True to form, Dostoevsky challenges this new literary leader. Dostoevsky's first world-famous work, *Notes from Underground* (1864), undermines this Chernyshevsky's novel without the admiration that characterizes his emulation of Pushkin and Gogol.

We have touched on the rich past of the psychological novel in the eighteenth and later centuries, but it goes on being dis-invented by ideologues and goes on having to be reinvented by their opponents because the subtleties of psychology defy most ideologies. As is frequently asserted, Dostoevsky reacted against the sensationalist sexual and social doctrines and the utopian and utilitarian politics of *What Is to Be Done?*, but he also reacted against it novelistically in the realm of causality. For Chernyshevsky, events are linked to one another by a clear sense that certain human beings are in control of their destinies, that possession of a strong will and correct ideas would enable human beings to reshape their lives or the whole world for the better. Much has been written about the influence of Nietzsche on the Nazis, but scholars have only begun to realize the impact of Nietzsche's thinking upon the Communists, partly because Bazarov, Rakhmetov, Sanin, and other characters from nineteenth-century Russian novels had already brought essentially Nietzschean values into the literary world the old Bolsheviks were brought up in.

Chernyshevsky saw little need to explain his characters psychologically because he viewed them as social types. Let us consider the scene where Chernyshevsky's narrator asks what sort of a person the hero, Lopakhin, is. The narrator answers that Lopakhin is the kind of person who, impoverished and dressed in rags, refuses to give way to a domineering and self-satisfied officer he meets striding down the street. Instead, Lopakhin picks the man up, casts him into a muddy ditch and threatens to drag him through it, then pulls him up, behaves as if the man has had an accident, and sends him on his way. Novelistically, Dostoevsky reacts angrily against the fact that Lopakhin fulfills the needs of Chernyshevsky's egalitarian politics and theories of universal human dignity, but has no psyche or inner motivation. Chernyshevsky invented a literary character in modern times that would bother to defend his right of way on the sidewalk and be greatly concerned with his costume while doing so. Robin Hood in merry England or Tybalt in fair Verona might care, of course, but a nineteenth-century Russian who worried about his dignity that much in that way would have to be very strange. Dostoevsky in response invented a man so insignificant that he tended to be ignored, and so insecure about existing at all that he constantly—offensively—demanded attention. The Underground Man challenges Chernyshevsky's doctrines in many ways, but the childishness of his psychology challenges the whole idea of writing a novel made up of exemplary characters and exemplary actions but lacking anything Dostoevsky would consider an inward life. For the Underground Man, giving way on the street acquires an enormity whose very morbidity draws attention to Lopakhin's lack of any psychology at all.

Chernyshevsky might ignore the psyche and isolate the social motives of his heroes, but Dostoevsky could not ignore the social; he had to realize that most of our actions emerge from the interplay between our social and our psychological identities, but as a novelist he discovered several ways of exploring the psyche in isolation from the social. The Underground Man theorizes about determinism and its implication that our actions were entirely external in origin—that we only react like piano keys, as predictably as logarithms—but he counters this with the assertion that in reality we often act contrary to our external interests, or even ignore them completely. This assertion of the gratuitous opens an area where a novelist can explore the psyche in pure action, undiluted by reaction. In the language of Émile Zola's later essay "Le roman experimental" (1880), the gratuitous act allows a novelist to conduct this part of his experiment with pure chemicals and reveal the true nature of a given character's psyche. Dostoevsky uses the probe of the gratuitous to explore the identity of his unreasonable characters, the first of whom is Goliadkin, the hero of his second novel *The Double*. Goliadkin sometimes responds to the words or actions of his colleagues in the office or of his doctor, but we learn the most about him when he simply surveys his nose, charters a carriage, walks into a store and buys nothing, or ruinously crashes a party, These actions are uncaused, thus outlining the extraordinary concern with his appearance that enables the illusion, the reality, or the practical joke of a double to destroy him. For other characters, gratuitous acts may be rare, but they reveal the psyche with the same clarity.

The Double was attacked for imitating Gogol, but Dostoevsky probably derived its causal system more from the tales and novels of Hoffmann. He once told his wife that the idea of this novel was the best he had ever had, and though he republished all his early works many times, *The Double* is the only one he bothered to rewrite many years later, reducing such eighteenth-century elements as letters and elaborate chapter titles. We do not know exactly what the word "idea" meant in his remark, but his intellect worked novelistically far better than it did systematically. In the plot of this novel, the disintegrating Goliadkin has a series of experiences whose causes could take many shapes. The arrival of an office colleague with an identical name could be explained as a strange coincidence, a practical joke, a supernatural event, or the delusion of a perception sinking into madness. Dostoevsky provides strong evidence for each of these plots and no basis for selecting among them, so that the cognitive dissonance drives the reader towards a disintegration very like Goliadkin's.

In *Crime and Punishment*, the murder is overdetermined; we know of Raskolnikov's poverty, his reaction to his sister's engagement to Luzhin, his superstitious reaction to a chance encounter with the idea of a murder like the one he is contemplating, his longing to be one of the elite who are eligible for crime, and so on, but the Raskolnikov who emerges at the end of the novel plans a marriage with a dying girl and runs into a burning building to rescue children he does not know.

These gratuitous acts reveal Raskolnikov more clearly than the caused ones. They also reveal an interesting difference between Dostoevsky and Freud. For Freud, the unconscious lacks the ability to analyze and moralize. In *Crime and Punishment*, the unconscious is deeply moral; Raskolnikov's dreams and impulsive actions struggle against his rational mind's rejection of moral values. There is nothing original in Dostoevsky's use of the gratuitous for the exploration of unusual psychologies. Poe, Laclos, Honoré de Balzac, and countless others had used it before him. But he made it a major instrument for investigating one of the key elements of psychology, which Poe had called "the perverse" and Dostoevsky called "the paradoxical."

A second way of exploring a psyche outside the realm of caused actions and reactions is to place characters in a position of total helplessness where nothing they do will make any difference. What one does at such a moment expresses one's pure identity. Marmeladov places himself in such a position, and asks Raskolnikov, "Have you ever known, Sir, what it is to have nowhere to turn?" (pt. 1, chap. 2). The Gentle Creature marries the horrible pawnbroker when the alternative is the same. The child Stavrogin rapes and the abused children Ivan Karamazov describes all experience this total helplessness, which enables them to express suicidal despair, faith in a child's God, or whatever else constitutes the center of the identity Dostoevsky has created for them. A major character like Mitya Karamazov reveals his particular pattern of dependency and childlike credulity when he visits Kuzma Samsonov and Madame Khokhlakova at a moment when there is absolutely no chance that they or anybody else would offer him the money to save what is left of his honor. Such situations raise central questions about the Dostoevskian plot, because the driving force of the fabula is normally cause and effect, and in these situations, actions are taken with no cause.

We have observed that motivation differs from other causation because it operates independently of time. The cause of an action may be an anticipated result rather than an action already taken, but in hopeless or gratuitous situations, the cause is explicitly removed, something that can happen in fiction, though not in history. History claims that events occurred, and in some cases it may assert that their causes are unknown, but in fiction, an unknown or assertedly nonexistent cause is not just unknown but simply not there. One can, of course write a book like *The Girlhood of Shakespeare's Heroines*, which is not a work of literary criticism but a work of art about other works of art, but we can never know why Mitya Karamazov's mother married old Fyodor. The text that calls her action gratuitous is the only arbiter on that issue.

Chernyshevsky did not drive Dostoevsky to reinvent the psychological novel, but *Notes from Underground* and *Crime and Punishment* are part of an ongoing sequence. Pushkin, Lermontov, Gogol, and Chernyshevsky, when each was the most celebrated prose experimenter in Russia, described the deeper motives of their characters briefly, if at all. Dostoevsky challenged them all by psychologizing their causal systems.

17

The Siuzhet of Part I of *Crime and Punishment* Programs the Reader to Read the Rest and to Participate Actively in a Vicious Murder

The plot that emerges in *Crime and Punishment* reflects much of Dostoevsky's background in the history of literature as well as his own evolution as a novelist. Part I of the novel can be isolated for a moment and studied as a novella called *Crime* whose much longer sequel would be called *Punishment*. This book begins with a rich depiction of the hero's alienation from the educational, economic, social, and moral worlds; it ends with him committing a murder. The second and third chapters contain two long embedded narratives: Marmeladov's monologue in the tavern and the letter from Raskolnikov's mother describing Dunya's trials as a governess for the Svidrigailovs and her engagement to Luzhin. These accounts contain much of the background of the novel, but in the construction of the causal system, Dostoevsky has given Raskolnikov no part in the events Marmeladov relates and little influence on the events in his mother's letter except for his absence and his need for money, about which his mother's account is silent. Except when Raskolnikov is involved, these two sets of events and characters continue to have little effect on one another, although Dostoevsky foregrounds Dunya's courtesy to Sonya Marmeladova and uses Svidrigailov's fortune to provide for the Marmeladov children. Luzhin persecutes

Sonya partly for political, partly for prurient, purposes, but primarily to offend and discredit Raskolnikov. But this lack of causal interconnection forces Dostoevsky to emphasize two other kinds of relationship between the Marmeladov fabula and the Svidrigailov-Dunya fabula. One is spatial: Svidrigailov lives adjacent to Sonya, and Luzhin lives among the other Marmeladovs.

Far more important are the parallels between the Marmeladov and the Dunya plots. Dunya's plan to sacrifice her happiness to support her brother's career is one of his strongest motives for the murder, and in one of the most puzzling passages in the novel, Raskolnikov tells Sonya that he had planned to confess the crime to her even before he had met her. To remind his readership of this organizing principle, parallelism, Dostoevsky begins the next chapter, the fourth in the novel, with a five-page interior monologue that is primarily Raskolnikov's literary criticism of his mother's letter, partly of its diction, use of the word "apparently," etc., but also of its plot, particularly the motivations of Luzhin, Dunya, and his mother. This third monologue in the novel ends with a comparison of the other two, an eloquently bitter linking of Sonya and Dunya: "Oh, dear and unjust hearts! ... Sonechka, Sonechka Marmeladova, the eternal Sonechka, as long as the World lasts! ... Do you know, Dunechka, that Sonechka's destiny is in no way more vile than a destiny with Mr. Luzhin?" (pt. I, chap. 4). Dostoevsky is using Raskolnikov to instruct his readers in how to read the relationship among the incidents in *Crime and Punishment*. Causation is important, and certainly time and space are, but as Raskolnikov forces us to see at this point, the Dunya plot is related to the Sonya plot centrally by analogy. Calculated marriages have been compared to prostitution by characters in Dickens, Hugo, George Sand, and other favorites of Dostoevsky's, but the nagging attention to the parallel constitutes one of the central elements of the Sonya plot. Of the five ways incidents can be related in a novel like *Crime and Punishment*, parallelism has probably received the most admiring attention. For Shakespeare, we have studied how parallelism leads to abstraction, or rather how it makes abstraction concrete by enabling readers to see and feel the common features for themselves. In *Crime and Punishment*, the multitude of parallelisms carries much of the ideological argument that drove Dostoevsky to write this particular novel at this time.

Chapter 4 continues with Raskolnikov meeting a disheveled teenager staggering down the boulevard. Raskolnikov reflects that her destiny is also prostitution and death before she is twenty, and he calls the hovering lecher "Svidrigailov," creating a cluster of three helpless women sacrificed to the lust of moneyed selfishness. By calling our attention to this "situation rhyme," Dostoevsky makes us see the consistency in Raskolnikov's responses to the three women. With Sonya's family, his first impulse is generous; he places money on the windowsill as he leaves, then in a fit of *esprit de l'escalier*, repents cynically on the staircase: "They have Sonya" (pt. 1, chap. 2). With Dunya, his first reaction to the Luzhin engagement is spirited. He wants to prevent the marriage, but then angrily asks himself what right he has to forbid it, which leads him to thoughts about murdering the pawnbroker. With the drunken teenager, he gives a policeman money to help her home, then calls to the puzzled policeman to forget the whole idea, telling himself that statistics prove that a certain percentage of women have to be ruined every year. By the end of the fourth chapter, therefore, Dostoevsky has trained his readers to expect parallel events producing parallel responses, and specifically to expect Raskolnikov to alternate between impulsive generosity and cynical afterthought. By the fifth chapter, the character of this alternation becomes clearer because it is laid out in Raskolnikov's interior monologue: "After *that*," he cried, springing from the bench, "but is *that* really going to happen? Can it be that it will happen?" (Pt. 1, chap. 5).

Earlier, the italicized words had been part of an authorial strategy to inspire *curiosité*, the reader's drive to figure out what is going on, but by now it is clear to the reader that "*that*" refers to the murder; the italicized words are a part of Raskolnikov's system for tabooing explicit enunciation of the principal matter on his mind. By the end of the fifth chapter, Dostoevsky has laid out the chief algorithm for creating or interpreting *Crime and Punishment*—the alternation in Raskolnikov's mind between two fully established bodies of imagery and ideology:

dream (*son*) vs. daydream (*mechta*)
unconsciousness vs. consciousness
impulse vs. afterthought
generosity vs. economics

religion vs. mathematics

nature vs. science

humanity vs. statistics

intuition vs. reason

freedom vs. burden (*bremia*)

air vs. enslavement

revulsion vs. murder

After the murder, more elements enter the picture, notably the opposition between confession and suicide and between resurrection and death, but by the end of the fifth chapter, the plan for the novel is in place, and it is daringly simple.

The plot of *Crime and Punishment* has its main action within the mind of Raskolnikov. He is on stage almost all the time, usually as a central actor, but sometimes, as in chapters 2 and 3, as the audience for the account of another character. When he is not on stage, one of his two surrogates, Razumikhin or Svidrigailov, usually occupies our attention. In this sense, Dostoevsky has abandoned the plot of the letter novel, in which two or more narrators can see the same event. We know that Dostoevsky first planned to narrate the novel in the first person, through Raskolnikov's eyes and voice. But first-person narration never worked as well for Dostoevsky in full-length novels as it did in his greatest shorter works, probably for technical reasons: the need for eavesdropping, letters, or outside reports to inform a narrator cut off from authorial omniscience. But the obsessive, sometimes oppressive involvement in Raskolnikov's life survived the shift to third-person narration.

Critics often call Raskolnikov unpredictable and the novel tormentingly disorienting, just as they call Moscow's Cathedral of the Blessed Basil wild and violent. But the power of that cathedral rests in part on the rigid formality of its floor plan, and the power of *Crime and Punishment* rests in part on the clarity of the central split, or *raskol*, in Raskolnikov's mind and its enactment in alternating states of mind, often separated by the word *vdrug*, "suddenly."

Once he has trained us to expect this algorithm, Dostoevsky sets to work to implicate us in the crime. He ends chapter 4 by setting up a parallel for Raskolnikov, embedding a brief portrait of Razumikhin, another ex-student, but one who is companionable, practical, cheerful, and simple-hearted, as opposed to Raskolnikov, who is a loner, unable or unwilling to help himself, grim, haughty, and excessively intellectual. In exactly the same position, they are heading in opposite directions. Next, Dostoevsky introduces the first great scene in the novel, again an embedded one—a dream. In this dream, we see another moment in Raskolnikov's background, his childhood when his father was alive, seeing it again with Raskolnikov as spectator at two levels, adult spectator to the dream and child spectator to the beating of the horse within the dream. This double layering involves us with Raskolnikov, whose impulses at both ages coincide with our own, and the vividness of the dream—its play on personal power, personal possession of a living female creature, savage glee in that possession and in the destructive use of it—all link this passage with the passages about Luzhin, Svidrigailov, and the lecher passing the ruined teenager on the boulevard. Our experience of Raskolnikov's experience retains its obsessive integrity.

The aftermath of this dream near the end of chapter 5 repeats the paired bodies of imagery and ideology that we have already assimilated but may not have noticed as organized polar oppositions until now:

He wants to catch his breath, cry out, and wakes up . . . all in a sweat, his hair drenched with sweat, gasping, and sat up in horror.

"Thank God, it's just a dream," he said . . . taking a deep breath. . . . "Isn't this a fever starting up in me, such a hideous dream". . . .

"Oh, God, . . . Can it be, can it really be that I will take an axe and start beating her head, and smash her skull—will slip on sticky, warm blood, smash a lock, steal and tremble, hide, all bloodied—with an axe—Lord, can it be? . . .

"No, I won't endure it, I won't. Suppose, suppose there's not even any doubt at all in all these calculations, suppose that all that's been decided this month were clear as day, fair as arithmetic. Lord! I still would not decide to do it." . . . He suddenly breathed more easily. He felt that he already had cast off this fearsome burden that had been crushing him so long, and his heart suddenly grew light and was at peace. "Lord, show me my way, and I renounce this damned—daydream of mine."

> Crossing the bridge, he gazed quietly and peaceably at the Neva, at the brilliant setting of a bright red sun. . . . It was as if a boil on his heart that had been swelling all month had suddenly burst. Freedom! Freedom! He was free now from these hexes, these enchantments, these obsessions.   (pt. I, chap. 5)

This passage is so powerful that most readers probably form a new expectation at this point to replace the alternation they have been trained to expect. The fate of that new expectation is the subject of a later chapter, but here we will turn to the end of part I, after Raskolnikov has done exactly what he envisioned with such revulsion in the passage just quoted.

Raskolnikov—whose actions, passions, and experiences we have shared without interruption (waking, sleeping, listening, and committing murder)—has unhooked the door and listened at the stairhead, waiting patiently to escape. He hears voices in the distance, then silence, then the noisy painters quitting work, and then someone's footsteps approaching, heavily, evenly, unhurriedly. He freezes, as in a nightmare when one dreams pursuers are catching up, closing in, wanting to kill, and it's as if one has taken root there and can't move one's hands. He finally slips back to the pawnbroker's room, rehooks the door, and hides, not breathing. As Raskolnikov stands in the room with the two bleeding corpses, holding his breath as he listens at the door, inches from his potential discoverers, who may leave or summon the police, we readers hold our breath, exert our will upon him not to give up and confess, and then suddenly realize that we are accessories after the fact, trying to help this merciless, calculating hatchet-murderer to escape.

This complicity in the crime alternates with the reader's horror and revulsion at it, just as Raskolnikov alternates between a drive towards murder and escape and a drive toward freedom from the murderous impulse and—after the murder—towards confession. Dostoevsky's siuzhet manipulates his readers into the fabula of the novel by almost never letting them outside the mind of Raskolnikov. We have mentioned that this intensity of narrative concentration on a single figure implicates the readers in his predicament much as readers willed the escape of picaresque scamps in earlier novels. *Crime and Punishment* has a beginning, a middle, and an end, but it retains the algorithmic integrity of

Gogol and his masters. In *Crime and Punishment*, the shaping rule is not accretive and perverse as in *Dead Souls*, but is rather the terrifying alternation between the crime and the punishment, the rational calculation that the destruction of a bloodsucking insect was an action worthy of a great man and the direct, emotional realization that this was the murder of a helpless fellow human being. Dostoevsky uses his narrative tools to draw the reader inside this vacillation.

By constructing a siuzhet that makes us live with his protagonist so intimately for ninety pages, Dostoevsky has implicated us in a crime that is vicious, greedy, cold, and despicable. This is the manipulative novel at its strongest. It tells us what is happening, shows us what is happening, but more than that, it makes us experience what is happening. From the end of part I, the reader, like Raskolnikov, will alternate between a strong drive towards his escape and a drive toward his confession. The siuzhet programs the reader's experience to track the hero's experience in the fabula.

18

The One-Sidedness of Desire and Violence in *Crime and Punishment* Is More Peculiar to Dostoevsky's Plotting Than *Dostoevshchina*

Psychology in Dostoevsky is often linked to that special quality the Russians call *Dostoevshchina*. It involves gloom, suffering, self-will, self-pity, hysteria, and other exaggerated and sometimes pathological emotions that often appear in Dostoevsky's fiction. Curiously, these elements are among the least unique in Dostoevsky's work. They are the stock in trade for the most popular prose writers of the nineteenth century: Hoffmann, Dickens, Hugo, and all the Gothic and Sensationalist novelists of that period, particularly Poe, who is often called the inventor of the detective story and whom Dostoevsky, as a publisher and editor, introduced to Russian readers.

Certain patterns, however, are genuinely peculiar to Dostoevsky and deserve more psychological and literary study than they have received. Let us consider violence, for example. There is no shortage of it. In *Crime and Punishment* alone, Aliona and Lizaveta have their skulls bashed in; a landlady is seriously beaten in one dream and a horse beaten to death in another; Marmeladov's wife hauls him about by his hair and slams his forehead against the floor; an angry coachman catches Raskolnikov with his whip; Razumikhin knocks a watchman off his feet; a trades-woman, an abused child, and Svidrigailov all attempt suicide, the last two successfully; and in Raskolnikov's final dream, the entire world is engulfed in lucidly self-righteous violence. Curiously, however, all this violence does not include a single good fight. With the exception of the completely abstract slaughter in the final dream, every one of these attacks is one-sided. The nearest thing to a fair fight in *Crime and Punishment* is the scrap between the two painters after a day's work together: "I grabbed Mitka by the hair and knocked him down and started tearing at him, and Mitya grabbed me by the hair, from under me, and started tearing at me, and we did this not in anger, but in all affection, in play" (pt. 2, chap. 4). Lizaveta does not even raise her hand to deflect the axe, and Marmeladov, who assisted his wife's efforts, looks up from the floor and tells Raskolnikov that this beating brings him satisfaction, *naslazhdeniie* (pt. 1, chap. 2).

Plainly, however, this one-sidedness in violence does not come from any inherent inability of Dostoevskian characters to resist aggression, or any universal masochism. As his journalistic career shows, Dostoevsky himself was good at reciprocating hostility. In his works, the number of two-sided contests at the verbal level is at least equal to the number of beatings on the physical level. Raskolnikov insults Razumikhin, Porfiry, and the explosive lieutenant at the police station, and all of them give as good as they get. Luzhin and Svidrigailov respond to Raskolnikov's insults with greater restraint or irony, but they certainly could never be called submissive like Lizaveta or compliant like Marmeladov. In this novel, and in general in Dostoevsky, if violence is reciprocal, it is not physical; if it is physical, it is not reciprocal. The reverse of these statements does not hold true. If an assault is not physical, it may or may not be reciprocated: Razumikhin does not always answer Raskolnikov's verbal assaults, and Sonya never does. If an assault is not reciprocated, it may or may not be physical: Marmeladov welcomes verbal as well as physical assaults.

Readers often remark how few happily married husbands and wives there are in Dostoevsky, although he himself was a devoted and loving family man. In her Columbia doctoral dissertation, Rima Shore points out that in *Crime and Punishment* the two unhappy couples, the Marmeladovs and the Svidrigailovs, are all dead by the end of the novel, and that Raskolnikov confesses to the only surviving father, the explosive lieutenant, rather than to the emphatically unmarried Porfiry, as one might otherwise expect. This absence of happy marriages might be ascribed to a novelistic tradition that marries characters off only at the end of the book, after a series of impediments and travails that constitute the plot of the novel. In Dostoevsky, however, there is virtually no good clean sex outside of marriage either, and the novelistic tradition of his day certainly accepted that. The absence of happy marriages and healthy extramarital sex might be ascribed to prudery, but that explanation will not work either because in many of Dostoevsky's novels there is no shortage of depraved sex, which is subject to stricter taboos. In *Crime and Punishment*, Svidrigailov rapes a little girl and someone like him misuses the girl Raskolnikov tries to rescue on the street; Sonya and the prostitutes near Raskolnikov's apartment earn their living through the loveless and eventually fatal selling of their bodies to satisfy desire.

This limitation of sexual encounters to depraved characters persists in all of Dostoevsky's stories and novels. It is hard to find happy marriages or mutually fulfilling sex in any of Dostoevsky's works. But this limitation does not come from any Dostoevskian hostility to marriage or love. Razumikhin and Dunya are two of the liveliest and loveliest lovers in all of literature, and Raskolnikov and Sonya save each other through their love, but these loves go unconsummated until the epilogue, as tends to happen with the happy love in all Dostoevsky's other works.

There are many definitions of depravity, but for the purposes of this chapter, I should like to define it as consummated but unreciprocated desire. This definition leads to a puzzle that demands attention. In Dostoevsky's novels, desire, like aggression, if physically consummated is not reciprocated, and if reciprocated is not consummated. As with violence, this pattern does not work backwards; unreciprocated desire may be either unconsummated, like Luzhin's, or physical, like that of Sonya's customers; while unconsummated desire may be reciprocated, like Razumikhin's for Dunya, or unreciprocated, like Luzhin's. In short, in two apparently unrelated regions of Dostoevsky's oeuvre—desire and violence—if it is physical, it is not reciprocal, and if it is reciprocal, it is not physical.

This pattern has at least four possible explanations. Socially, in a society like Russia's, where some people owned others, the consummation of unreciprocated desire becomes a part of interclass rather than interpersonal relations and may radiate from that center throughout the society. And in a society where the gentry dreaded the corporal powers of the tsarist bureaucracy, as Irina Reyfman has pointed out, single combat became a defining prerogative of the gentry, who go practically unrepresented in *Crime and Punishment* and is underrepresented in most of Dostoevsky's works. This pair of explanations might play a small part in explaining the number of beatings and depraved sexual encounters, but it is of little use in explaining the absence of fights or sexual mutuality, both of which transcend all social limitations.

Psychologically, Dostoevsky may well have believed that in sex one partner was always stronger, more sophisticated, and in a position to exploit the more innocent and weaker. Evgeny Opochinin records him as saying this, and his sense that his sister Varvara was victimized by her older, richer husband fused with much of his reading of Sand, Thomas De Quincey, the Gothic novelists, and all the heirs of Richardson to generate a pervasive picture of exploitative physical love, sometimes reciprocated at a comparable level, as Samsonov's practical affection for Grushenka seems to be in *The Brothers Karamazov*, but often depraved, like Bykov's for Varvara in *Poor Folk*. Dostoevsky's psychological vision certainly paid due attention to the phenomenon of dominance by the strong and submissiveness by those who must submit. His psychology of desire may have simply amplified this awareness into a universal pattern. With violence, however, this pattern does not work at all. In fact, the weaker often assault the stronger, who do not reciprocate. Neither Marmeladov nor Fedor Karamazov and Maksimov in *The Brothers Karamazov* are weaklings, but they are physically beaten by their wives. Here we are dealing with some sort of moral dominance that does not fall within the traditional range of psychological inquiry.

If both a psychological and a social explanation seem inadequate for this mutual exclusion of the physical and the reciprocal, a literary explanation remains worth exploring. The novelistic tradition emerges from earlier traditions of unrequited or unfulfilled love. Greek romance left its heroes physically victimized and their love unconsummated until an epilogic moment. Medieval romance tended to do the same, as did later novels which Bakhtin characterizes as ordeal novels. The Dunya/Razumikhin subplot in *Crime and Punishment* follows this Bakhtinian formula. The strikingly beautiful woman undergoes dangers and indignities in her economic and social life before an epilogic union with a brave, enduring man who has been infatuated with her from the beginning. Long before Bakhtin, in the first lines of book 1, canto 3, of *The Faerie Queene*, Edmund Spenser describes the power of such plots to stimulate one of the two emotions Aristotle expected of dramatic plots:

> Nought is there under heav'ns wide hollownesse,
> That moves more deare compassion of mind,
> Then beautie brought t' unworthie wretchednesse
> Through envies Snares, or fortunes freakes unkind.

> (1.3.1–4)

But pity is only one of Dostoyevsky's novelistic goals. A beating or a one-sided assault can produce a moral sense of wrong being done, while a fair fight stimulates very different emotions. The assaults in Dostoevsky and the consummation of depraved desire can both appeal to our moral indignation in ways that a fair fight or happy love cannot. This is the spirit not of the ordeal but of melodrama, in which the goodness of the victim, more than the beauty and worthiness, involves the readership in the story. At every step of a literary plot, it is helpful to have a wrong that needs to be righted. The reader desires justice, and whether the siuzhet satisfies that desire or not, the reader continues to turn the pages. This explanation works for much of the violence and the depraved love in Dostoevsky, but not all of it. Raskolnikov's encounters with the abused girl or the prostitutes on the street have marks of closure which make them too episodic to produce any reader expectations at all. The majority of the assaults on Fedor Karamazov seem eminently satisfying, and Marmeladov certainly deserves the treatment his wife gives him, although it may not work as negative reinforcement.

To seek a solution to this puzzle about the parallel structures of desire and violence in Dostoevsky, let us turn to one of the many moments when these two elements share the stage: Dunya's visit to Svidrigailov in his apartment. In the past Svidrigailov has been both the victim and the beneficiary of Marfa Petrovna's unreciprocated desire, selling himself much as Sonya does professionally and as Dunya has tried to do as the victim and beneficiary of Luzhin's unreciprocated desire. Svidrigailov has tried to exploit his lordly provincial power over Dunya, but her Sandean spiritedness has, as he puts it, "done more harm to me than I to you, even in the country" (pt. 6, chap. 5). Now he has the new power of blackmail over her, threatening to denounce her brother as a murderer; in addition, as he himself points out, he is twice as strong as she is, in a completely isolated apartment, a standard location for melodramatic victimization. Svidrigailov is not Luzhin; for him, power is an instrument of lust, not an object of it, but he is prepared to use it ruthlessly until Dunya pulls a revolver on him, to which he responds, "Well, that altogether changes the course of events." Certainly, as Mao Zedong and Davy Crockett knew, a revolver does alter the power relationship. Rape might at first seem to be the place where desire and violence meet most clearly, but rape seems to be motivated by power more often than by desire. The assault on Dunya that Svidrigailov contemplated may be exceptional in using violence for the sake of desire and not of power. He continues, however, "You are simplifying the matter extraordinarily, Avdotya Romanovna." "The matter" is probably not Svidrigailov's anticipated suicide; the decision on that is not final until after Dunya rejects him definitively.

Rather, he is stating that his newly acquired weakness gives him some power over Dunya, just as her powerlessness in the provinces coupled with a little bit of luck gave her the power to reject him. Indeed, with a little bit of luck and the power of helplessness, he turns her unreciprocated assault with a gun into a complete defeat when she casts the revolver aside, returning herself to helplessness. At this point, she regains that same power she had possessed in the provinces. He puts his arm around her waist and she beseechingly says, "Let me go!" He trembles and asks, "So you don't love me?" She shakes her head, and he whispers, in despair, "And . . . you can't, ever?" When she answers, "Never," he lets her go. Here, we have desire which may at some point have been reciprocated; the text offers no hard evidence to support either Dunya's angry denial or Svidrigailov's insinuating assertion. Since his wife's death, in any case, his desire has been entirely unreciprocated, and only power can lead to its physical consummation. But power in this scene works backwards, as it tends to work in Svidrigailov's life. He kills the wife who holds power over him and the people he kills all haunt him, much as Lizaveta and the old pawnbroker haunt Raskolnikov, from the total powerlessness of death. If power forms the link that explains the parallel mechanisms of violence and desire in Dostoevsky, it is more often than not paradoxical power. The beaten and the sexually exploited inherit the earth. In both these cases the power of weakness becomes central. I would suggest that the unifying element that explains the incompatibility of the reciprocal and the physical may well be this paradox of power in these two areas, desire and aggression. For Dostoevsky, victims become victors. If tragedy is about the weakness of the strong, novels—or at least this kind of novel—are about the power of the weak.

This insight was not original with Dostoevsky; Jesus, for example, came to it earlier, and Dostoevsky was deeply Christian. But Dostoevsky's contribution to the history of psychology does not lie in the originality of his discoveries. It lies in the way he brought the insights of his time (and of Jesus's, and Sophocles's too) before the kind of reader who passionately intellectualizes a fictional world. He made the psychological novel a philosophical instrument by using parallel plots to explore the ways characters' ideas about the world were related to their personalities and their relationships to power. His ideas feel original because he carries us through the process of discovering them.

And because his novelistic, religious, social, and psychological imperatives each reinforced all the others, he could control all of the elements in his fiction to achieve the integrity of impact that made his vision of humanity particularly contagious. He made us feel that psychology is part of the novelistic whole.

19

Critics Often Attack *Crime and Punishment* for a Rhetoric That Exploits Causality in Ways They Misunderstand

The causal relationships in the fabula of *Crime and Punishment* have had a bad press. One of the most common observations about the novel challenges the number of coincidences, chance meetings, and episodes of eavesdropping it contains. Ernest Simmons summed up a large body of opinion in 1947 when he wrote,

> Coincidence is an ever-present trap for weary novelists, and in this respect Dostoevsky nodded rather frequently in *Crime and Punishment*. It is perhaps the principal artistic blemish in the work. Coincidence, of course, may be justifiable in a novel, for it is a legitimate part of the pattern of reality. In real life, however, coincidental happenings do not violate the laws of probability, and in fiction our credibility is forfeited if coincidence is overworked. Dostoevsky certainly carries the matter too far in *Crime and Punishment*. Svidrigailov hears the reply which significantly affects the action. Lebeziatnikov bumps into Raskolnikov on the crowded city streets just when he is looking for him. . . . Luzhin lives in the same house as the Marmeladovs, and Svidrigailov hires quarters in Sonya's house. The restricted stage, which recalls the misdirected application of

the unities in some bad imitations of classical drama, results in forced situations and unbelievable coincidences.

(Dostoevsky, 87–88)

Authorial fatigue as the explanation for literary fact has great commonsense appeal. When Homer is weary, he nods. Like coincidence for fiction writers, however, fatigue offers critics a dangerously easy way to solve problems, and it may empathetically occur most often to a weary critic. Like Homer, Dostoevsky made many mistakes, but I owe it to my craft in each specific case to explore every possibility of purposefulness in the text. I have already argued that consistently following an algorithm without prescience can produce the same effect as advance structural planning. There is no question that Dostoevsky explicitly abandoned causation startlingly often in *Crime and Punishment*, and that these coincidences deserve attention.

Some incidents in the novel seem more strikingly coincidental today than they did in Dostoevsky's time. I used to be troubled by the provenance of the murder weapon in *Crime and Punishment*. Raskolnikov has carefully planned to use his landlady's ax, finds it unavailable, and then happens upon an ax in the porter's lodge. Plainly this is not a coincidence used by a weary author to solve a problem; if anything, Dostoevsky introduces a slightly clumsy problem in order to need the coincidence. It would have been easier to let Raskolnikov simply find the ax as planned and to do without the angry outburst of discouragement at the disruption of his plan and the strong reaction of encouragement at its reinstatement:

> He leaped headlong for the ax (it was an ax) and drew it from under the bench where it was lying between two logs; right there, without going out, he fastened it to the loop, put both hands in his pockets, and went out of the porter's lodge. No one had noticed. "If reason won't, the Devil will!" [*Ne rassudok, tak bes!*] he thought, laughing strangely. This occurrence encouraged him extraordinarily.
>
> (pt. I, chap. 6)

When I first went to Leningrad in 1956, I wandered through the apartment courtyards in the area Dostoevsky knew. All the yards were stacked with firewood. Suddenly I realized that *no* coincidence was needed to provide an ax. Axes were part of the landscape in those days.

Some of the other coincidences also relate to the real world Dostoevsky was describing. Raskolnikov's St. Petersburg is huge and oppressive, a city that goes on and on whenever Svidrigailov or Raskolnikov wander, and yet, as Simmons notes, the two chief villains each happen to rent rooms adjacent to Sonya, although their desires focus on Dunya, the other chief heroine. Raskolnikov happens upon the dying Marmeladov; Svidrigailov happens upon Raskolnikov. Raskolnikov even happens upon his best friend Razumikhin and crosses the street to avoid him, which Razumikhin observes and ignores, out of respect for Raskolnikov's privacy. This last coincidence is hardly a part of the fabula at all, since it has no cause or effect, happens in no time or place, and operates primarily to characterize Razumikhin and Raskolnikov.

Artistically, these and many other encounters enhance the oppressiveness of the setting. St. Petersburg becomes a city whose inhabitants cannot escape one another. In fact, the hugeness of St. Petersburg derives more from Dostoevsky's literary sources than from any reality he was depicting. In 1860, Dickens's London and Hugo's or Balzac's Paris had populations in the millions, but St. Petersburg had barely half a million; there was real country within a half hour's walk from any point in town. The poor were distributed more by the number of floors above the street than by neighborhoods, but the cluster of poor students, broken bureaucrats, and petty businesses in the nasty area where city met country at the hay barges made chance encounters appropriate parts of the everyday scene.

Yet even though some coincidences were less marked for Dostoevsky's earlier readers and others strengthened the oppressive urban atmosphere, many coincidences demand more serious literary attention. After his dream of the beaten horse, as we have already seen, Raskolnikov has definitively abandoned the idea of murdering the old pawnbroker and "suddenly began to breathe easier. He felt that he had already cast off this fearsome burden that had been crushing him so long," that he was liberated from some enchantment (pt. 1, chap. 5). On his way home, he makes an unnecessary detour through the Haymarket and happens to overhear a conversation indicating that the old pawnbroker will be alone at seven o'clock the next evening. In the world of ordinary causation, this information would have meant no more to Raskolnikov than to any other passerby. For a man who is no longer considering a murder, this coincidence would mean no more than it would to a man who has never considered a murder—that is to say, nothing at all. In the novel, however, Raskolnikov returns home "like a man condemned to death," unable to resist the drive to murder. Something has deprived him of the freedom which is associated with air and life.

At this point in the siuzhet, the narrator introduces an incident which occurred before the novel began, Raskolnikov's overhearing a conversation about murdering the pawnbroker:

> "One life and a thousand lives in return, that's sheer arithmetic! And on the universal balance, what does the life of this stupid, vicious, consumptive old crone mean? No more than the life of a louse, a cockroach, or not even that because the old crone is harmful. . . ."
>
> "Of course, she doesn't deserve to live . . . but that's how nature is."
>
> "Aw, old man, you know they fix nature up and guide it, and otherwise we'd have to drown in prejudices. Otherwise, there'd never have been a single great man. People talk about 'duty, conscience,' . . . But look at how we understand them."
>
> Raskolnikov was extraordinarily distraught. Of course, all this was the most commonplace and ordinary youthful conversation and thought; he'd heard it more than once before, in other forms, on other themes. But why exactly he had happened to hear exactly this conversation and such thoughts as had just been emerging in his own head. . . . *Just exactly these same thoughts.*

> (pt. 1, chap. 6)

Let us look at this passage under the categories we established in part 1 of this study. Chronologically, this incident is placed about six weeks before Raskolnikov overhears Lizaveta's conversation in the square. Geographically, it is placed in the kind of tavern that Raskolnikov rarely visits, but that Marmeladov and later Svidrigailov inhabit. In terms of parallelism, it is one of those rare cases where two incidents are identical, at least in Raskolnikov's mind as he compares his version of the murder with the student's. Identical events, or justifications for events, lie at the opposite end of a spectrum from those with nothing in common. In the realm of causation, this overheard conversation is already at the zero end of the spectrum in one sense, since Raskolnikov "happens" to hear it. On the other hand, this conversation is important among the causes of the murder. Dostoevsky's narrator carefully removes the possibility that the conversation gave Raskolnikov any information or conception. The conversation was commonplace and coincided *exactly* with an idea Raskolnikov was already hatching. The importance resided in one thing: the coincidence of encountering this idea at this moment. We have discussed the way the allegorical use of parallel plots lead readers to feel they are living in a universe God designed to work consistently. Coincidence here leads us to a sense of living in a universe the Devil designed capriciously. But caprice has its order, too.

The overhearing both of the student and of Lizaveta matters only because they are coincidences. In the second paragraph of chapter 6, we are told, "Always after that in this whole business, he tended to see some sort of a strangeness, as if in the presence of some special influences and coincidences." Coincidence here takes on a very special function. It solves absolutely no problem for a weary author. It introduces into the hero's set of motives a new causal mechanism, superstition. In the world of science, throwing salt over one's shoulder or sticking pins in an effigy causes very little to happen. In the world of superstition, both actions are purposeful because they are expected to be effective. In the first paragraph of chapter 6, Dostoevsky takes the trouble to give a circumstantial everyday explanation for Lizaveta's presence in the Haymarket, relating it to her work, though not to Raskolnikov's random, explicitly unmotivated decision to walk there. The next paragraph begins with the word "but," and introduces a word that was an important part of the intellectual world of the 1860s: "But Raskolnikov had grown superstitious of late. Traces of superstition remained in him long afterwards, almost ineradicably" (pt. 1, chap. 6). In Auguste Comte's vision of universal history, mankind moves through three stages: a stage of superstition, when men believe they can influence nature through secret procedures; a stage of religion, when men believe they can influence nature through the intervention of divinities; and a stage of science, when they actually can influence nature by understanding the laws by which it operates. The Russian Nihilists and all the Positivists prided themselves on residing in the final stage of intellectual history, and looked down on religious people as throwbacks to an earlier age. Dostoevsky delighted in mocking great and little scientific minds for operating not on reason but on faith. He felt considerable distaste for spiritualism, but attacked Dmitry Mendeleev in the January, March, and April 1876 issues of *Diary of a Writer* for claiming that spiritualism could not possibly be true and didn't need to be proven fraudulent. This was a statement of faith, not science.

Yet in the first paragraph of *Notes from Underground*, when the Underground Man can make no sense of his sickness, he goes on, "I'm taking no treatment, and never did, although I respect medicine and doctors. Moreover, I'm superstitious in the extreme; well, at least enough to respect medicine. I'm sufficiently educated not to be superstitious, but I'm superstitious" (1). The Underground Man is suggesting here that respect for medicine emerges from superstition, but Dostoevsky is hinting that many of his ideological foes—the positivists, scientists, materialists, and nihilists—have not superseded the religious stage in the history of humanity, but have in fact retreated to the superstitious stage. Dostoevsky is using coincidences to undercut the confidence of his adversaries in their control of the world to suggest that discovering a force at work in the world or a law of nature is little different from discovering that a hex produces a desired result. This is an attack not so much on science as on scientism, the belief that science can solve all problems, whether social, historical, or intellectual.

When he uses the word "but" to introduce the word "superstition" after giving a very everyday explanation for Lizaveta's presence, he is setting two parallel causal systems into operation, much as had been done by Lermontov, whom Dostoevsky called one of the two "demons" in Russian literature. The first system is the narrator's commonplace, everyday causal system, where people earn livings, go broke, put kinks into chronology when they make plans and appointments, but are living in the world that Dostoevsky's enemies called "real." The second system is Raskolnikov's sick, superstitious, strange way of relating incidents, which reads the finding of an everyday ax as extraordinarily encouraging, operating in a world of omens and proverbs like, "If reason won't, the devil will!" Dostoevsky uses many of the coincidences in the novel to slam his narrator's commonsense reading against Raskolnikov's sick, superstitious, but pseudo-rational reading of the same event. What works fictionally as melodramatic plotting works ideologically as argumentative plotting.

20

The Epilogue of *Crime and Punishment* Crystallizes Its Ideological Plot

Critics tend to treat epilogues as places at the end of novels where authors answer outstanding questions about their characters, put an end to trains of action, and distance the chief events of a novel enough to moderate the reader's emergence from the intensities of novelistic life. In his preface to *Roderick Hudson* (1875), Henry James calls this part of a novel "a distribution at the last of prizes, pensions, husbands, wives, babies, millions, appended paragraphs, and cheerful remarks" (quoted in "The Art of Fiction," 8). Frank Kermode cites the "conclusion" (*zakliucheniie*) of Dostoevsky's *Idiot* as a good example of the type of epilogue that James referred to. He certainly is right about *The Idiot*, with its use of a visit by the Epanchins to Myshkin as a chance to review the continuing careers of the other major characters. But Dostoevsky used many other kinds of epilogue, ranging through the conclusions of *The Friend of the Family* and *The Gambler* to the long narrative at the end of *The Insulted and Injured*, the only ending he calls an epilogue, except for the elaborate ones of *Crime and Punishment* and *The Brothers Karamazov*. *The Possessed* has three epilogues, none so labeled: the ambitious and circumstantial Stepan Trofimovich epilogue; the short account of the fates of the conspirators, which fits James's characterization; and the Stavrogin epilogue, which certainly does nothing to relax the intensity of the reader's experience. At the other end of the spectrum, Dostoevsky could write a novel like *Poor Folk* without an epilogue, and—I would argue—at least two epilogues without novels, the retrospective stories "The Gentle Creature," and "The Dream of a Ridiculous Man."

For more than a century, readers have objected to the epilogue of *Crime and Punishment* on the grounds of inconsistency with the rest of the novel. Simmons reflected a broad body of opinion in 1947 when he wrote: "The epilogue is manifestly the weakest section of the novel, and the regeneration of Raskolnikov under the influence of the Christian humility and the love of Sonya is neither artistically palatable nor psychologically sound. It would be interesting to know why Dostoevsky set aside the logic of events in rejecting the ending of suicide for his hero" (*Dostoevsky*, 153). Such attacks on the epilogue plainly reflect its departure from the character of the main text. For several hundred pages, Raskolnikov has wavered, first between murder and a rich subconscious array of generous and noble impulses, and then between confession and a strong scientistic array of social and psychological calculations. Suddenly in the epilogue, as the critical community has long observed, the novel loses this dialogic quality, which Bakhtin considers the center of the truly novelistic, and reads more like a devotional or inspirational tract, an account of conversion, repentance, and resurrection. The Raskolnikov who confesses to Sonya in a horrifying, allusive, almost wordless encounter, crudely asserts later, "I really only killed a louse, Sonya, a useless, nasty, harmful one" (pt. 5, chap. 5). But such torturous alternations end, and right before the end of the epilogue, "he remembered how constantly he had tortured and injured her heart, remembered her poor, thin little face, but now these recollections hardly tortured him; he knew with what endless love he would now redeem all her sufferings." This disappearance of the polyphonic may shock a good Bakhtinian in terms of the philosophy of the novel, but it fits Bakhtin's ideas about the history of the Dostoevskian plot. In the tradition that begins with Greek romances and evolves through medieval and Baroque accounts of adventures and ordeals into the Gothic novels and the traditions of Hoffman, Eugène Sue, and Balzac, Bakhtin expects the good-looking boy and girl of marriageable age to meet unexpectedly, suddenly become passionately involved, and encounter a series of obstacles that retard their union. After all these "attempts on chastity and fidelity, false accusations of crimes, . . . meetings with unexpected friends or enemies, . . . prophetic dreams . . . [etc.], the novel ends happily with the lovers united in marriage" (*The Dialogic Imagination*, 88).

Crime and Punishment is hardly a Greek romance, but Raskolnikov is the very image of his remarkably beautiful sister (pt. 3, chap. 1) and Sonya "was a small, eighteen-year-old, thin, but rather pretty blonde, with remarkable blue eyes" (pt. 2, chap. 6). Even where this prettiness is explicitly contradicted, it retains a shadowy presence: "She could not have been called pretty, but still her blue eyes were so clear, and when they lit up, the expression of her face became so kind and simple that you could not help being attracted to her" (pt. 3, chap. 4). In the fabula, Raskolnikov had suddenly become fixated on Sonya during Marmeladov's monologue in the second chapter of the novel, as we learn much later, at nearly the end of chapter 4 in part 4: "I had picked you out long since [to confess to] that time when your father was talking about you, and when Lizaveta was alive." She had become fixated upon him when he gave all he had to bury her father (pt. 3, chap. 4). Like the heroine of a Greek romance, Sonya is forced into prostitution, falsely accused of a crime, and separated from Raskolnikov by a prison sentence and a series of sicknesses, until in the second chapter of the epilogue, when they finally come together, and "in her eyes there shone infinite happiness: she understood, and for her there was no doubt that he loved her, infinitely, and that at last the moment had come." A Bakhtinian could argue, therefore, that in the history of literary genres, the epilogue of *Crime and Punishment* adheres consistently to a formula that shaped the plot of the novel as a whole, thus bringing it to the conclusion implicit in the genre. This account of *Crime and Punishment* as an ordeal novel makes historical sense, since Dostoevsky relished the nineteenth-century descendants of that tradition. Artistically, however, it does not explain why a novelist with subtle and intricate moral, psychological, religious, and political positions would select from all the novelistic traditions he knew one whose glory resided in its obsessive unsubtlety.

At one level, the argument that Raskolnikov repents only in the epilogue makes good religious sense. The contrast between his monologic repentance in the epilogue and the complex ambiguity of his confessions in the main text of the novel rises from the nature of confession in much Christian thinking. Confession is not the result of repentance. Rather, it is the means to it. *Crime and Punishment* has been described as a novel of multiple rehearsals followed by single performances and their aftermaths. In the opening scene, Raskolnikov rehearses the murder, bringing a real pledge in place of the dummy he will offer later on. He rehearses the murder again in his dream of the beating of the horse and a number of times in his conscious mind as he reflects about his plans. After the horrible, clumsy, botched performance, he begins rehearsing his confession, trying it out with great effect on Zametov at the Crystal Palace; in a fearsome, wordless scene with Razumikhin; in a dramatically unsuccessful kissing of the earth; and in the famous confession to Sonya. After all these rehearsals, he finally brings himself to confess to the explosive lieutenant at the police office. The aftermath of this successful confession is repentance and resurrection, which brings the novel to a close. When Raskolnikov confesses to Sonya, he cannot be expected to repent as of yet. This argument that the epilogue differs from the rest of the text because it describes a period after the achievement of confession offers a stronger explanation for the artistic nature of the epilogue than the historical tradition of Greek romance. But this doctrinal closure of the novel, destroying its dialogic power, seems to have troubled Dostoevsky himself. To reduce this closed feeling, he ends the novel narratively, offering the whole of it as the introduction to another story: "But this is where a new story begins, the story of the gradual renewal of a human being, the story of his gradual rebirth, gradual shift from one world to another, acquaintance with a new, hitherto altogether unknown reality. This could be the subject of a new account, but the present account is finished." This open end gives readers the sense of participation in an unfinished story.

Simmons's idea that suicide would have been the most logical outcome also occurs to Raskolnikov: "He suffered also from the thought of why he had not killed himself at that time. Why had he stood above the river then and given his preference to admitting the crime?" Dostoevsky offers two explanations for this decision, Raskolnikov's and the narrator's. Raskolnikov links it to the sheer love of life, and the narrator to the possibility that "even then, when he was standing above the river . . . he felt in his future and in that of his convictions a profound falsehood. He did not understand that this foreboding could be fore-warning of a future transformation in his life, his future resurrection." If the dialogue between these two answers to Simmons's question remains somewhat open, the dialogue in the novel as a whole throws important light on it. Basically two theories of crime collide in this novel. One is the theory Dostoevsky derived from Napoleon III's *History of Julius Caesar,* the belief that certain great figures are entitled to commit crimes with-out guilt or punishment because they will benefit humanity so greatly in their other activities. The other is Porfiry Petrovich's belief that crime is one of two symptoms of a disease whose other symptom is the need to get caught. Murderers therefore leave clues, visit the scene of the crime, spend the fruits of their crime conspicuously, tease the police, and—if all else fails—confess. If they do not, they commit suicide. When Raskolnikov tells Porfiry at the end of his last interrogation, "I have admitted nothing to you, remember that," Porfiry's answer is one of the great moments in the history of detective fiction:

> "Well, it goes without saying, I'll remember—why look, he's even trembling. Don't you worry, my sweetheart, thy will be done. Wan-der around a bit; only you mustn't wander too far. In any event, I do have one more big favor to ask of you," he added, lowering his voice. "A ticklish matter, but an important one: if in any event (which I don't believe will happen and consider quite against your nature)—in the event—well, in any event—if you should feel the inclination in these forty or fifty hours to finish the matter in some other way, in some fantastic manner—to inflict a bit of vio-lence on yourself (an absurd proposition, but, well, you must for-give me), then—leave a brief, but circumstantial note. That's it, two lines, just two bits of writing, and tell about the stone."
>
> (pt. 6, chap. 2)

Porfiry's hypnotically purposeful dithering emerges from his central doctrine. Bakhtin would argue that Dostoevsky's position emerges from the dialogue between these two theories of crime. I would argue that Dostoevsky appoints a judge to decide between the two doctrines: the plot. In the plot, he places Raskolnikov and a control, Svidrigailov. Each has killed two or maybe three people, since Lizaveta is often pregnant and does not raise her hand from a low protective position to defend her head. This is the kind of literary experiment Zola would propose a few years later. Raskolnikov confesses and is resurrected. Svidrigailov does not confess and commits suicide. Porfiry is fighting for law and order, but his affectionate comments should be taken literally, because he believes he is also fighting for Raskolnikov's life. In this way, while the discourse in *Crime and Punishment* leaps from the dialogic to the inspirational in the epilogue, the plot remains consistent with the whole, moving logically, though hesitantly, towards confession and then redemption.

The epilogue of *Crime and Punishment* can be treated as a work of art in its own right, achieving its extraordinary density of impact by relying on a massive prologue: the rest of the novel. This prologue loads the names, the events, and even certain words with meaning that enables Dostoevsky to address his readers with great economy of exposition after hundreds of pages spent training them. Let us examine the first paragraph of this work of art: "Siberia. On the shore of a broad wilderness river stands a city, one of the administrative centers of Russia; in the city is a fortress, in the fortress a prison camp. In the camp the transported second-class convict Rodion Raskolnikov has been imprisoned for nine months already. Almost a year and a half has passed since the day of his crime."

Dostoevsky can talk to us in shorthand because neither the crime nor the hero of this ten-page work of art needs any introduction, though Raskolnikov has acquired a new title to replace that of "student" with which he introduced himself to the pawnbroker and to his readership after several pages of anonymity in the first chapter of the novel, or the title "former student," which he uses more often. The one-word sentence "Siberia" eliminates *curiosité* from the siuzhet of this work of art, since a long tradition of transportation and exile has loaded that word with beauty, brutality, and a standardized repertory of landscapes and incidents. Dostoevsky's own *House of the Dead* had described the Omsk prison camp in rich detail. As Bakhtin would have expected, time is juxtaposed to place in this paragraph. Raskolnikov has been in Siberia nine months and had committed his crime a year and a half earlier. This is about average for a Dostoevsky epilogue, though *The Brothers Karamazov*, the novel most like *Crime and Punishment* in its epilogue, has only a five-day lapse. A year and eight months have elapsed before the last chapter of *The Gambler*, two years before that of *The Eternal Husband*, and six months before the conclusion of *The Raw Youth*.

After establishing a new time and place for this new work of art, one paragraph uses Raskolnikov's trial to review the story of his crime and a second paragraph describes the trial and sentencing, followed by the curious introduction of new material redounding to Raskolnikov's credit, adding materials to the fabula that reinforce the positive associations of impulsive as opposed to calculated actions. After this slightly abnormal epilogic material, the first chapter reverts to the format James formulated, recounting the destinies of Dunya, Sonya, Razumikhin, and Raskolnikov's mother. But critics of the novel object not so much to the rather conventional chapter 1 as to the far more powerful chapter 2 of the epilogue. The center of this chapter is Raskolnikov's final dream. Unlike the other dreams in *Crime and Punishment*, which are psychological and polysemous, the dream in the epilogue is as ideological as Chernyshevsky's dreams in *What Is to Be Done?* In this dream, the trichinae that infect the world are spirits (*dukhi*) endowed with mind and will: "People who have ingested them immediately become mad and insane. But never, never had human beings considered themselves so shrewd and unshakeable in the truth as did those infected. Never had they considered their pronouncements, their scientific conclusions, their moral convictions and beliefs more unshakeable. . . . People killed one another in some sort of mindless viciousness."

At this point in the epilogue, Dostoevsky brings the entire novel together. The social, historical, and scientific certainties that had led Raskolnikov to the murder are linked with the sicknesses from which he suffered through most of the novel. Porfiry's doctrine of crime as a sickness becomes linked with the idea of science as superstition, and these murderous microscopic spirits give a new meaning to Raskolnikov's bravado when he found the ax: "If reason won't, the Devil will" (pt. 1, chap. 6). The image of these diabolic microbes would evolve into the devils in the epigraph of *The Possessed* and into the polemic with Mendeleev and others over spiritualism in *The Diary of a Writer* a decade later, but at this point in Dostoevsky's career, it emerged as an unbelievably concise summation of the doctrine, imagery, and plotting of *Crime and Punishment*.

21

The Plots of Novels Teach Novelistic Justice, Not Poetic Justice

After many pages discussing what plots are, how they work, and what they can accomplish, it is time to address a final question, what plots mean, and the attendant hermeneutic question, how that meaning is knowable. For Plato, as we have mentioned, meaning often took the allegorical form we have described when we talked about parallelism. When he depicts the way a tyrant runs a Greek polity, he is also showing how a monomaniac runs his life, and he believes that the events in the state would unfold in a way that would unveil the more obscure events in the psyche. Plato apparently never saw any need to explain such correspondences.

For Plato, these correspondences may have emerged automatically from the sense that all examples of anything partook of an unchanging reality, or that the names of things arose from their identities. Others have found meaning in the overall feeling that a work of literature gives them, which turns the meaning of a text into a part of the autobiography of the reader. Positivists in the last century tried to prove that an *author* meant a given thing by quoting a *character* who had said it. Bakhtin's concept of polyphony drove out that approach by locating meaning in the interaction of the statements and the actions of the various characters, which again reduced the possibility of verifiability. In the 1970s, the New Nihilism aspired to deny the existence of any detectable meaning in a text, locating it in the views of a critic, or sometimes of a community of critics, and sometimes denying that there was any meaning to detect at all. This was almost a return to the early nineteenth-century commonplace that meaning was not even a desideratum: a poem should not mean but be. I should like to suggest that a plot can offer insight into the meaning of a text, and sometimes produce rather surprising insights.

Let me begin by making fun of the commonest way of finding meaning in a literary plot and then giving an example of a more serious argument. According to many of the most fashionable critics, plots can reveal the ideological position of the author in a very simple way. A review of the 1997 movie *Titanic* offers a good example:

> DeMille and his modern-day counterpart, James Cameron, portray working people as salt-of-the-earth types who frequently best their so-called "betters." This is evident in *Titanic*, where scenes show the working-class artist Jack Dawson triumphing over wealthy Cal Hockley in dinner conversation and in winning Rose DeWitt Bukater's love.
>
> Yet, beneath the liberal veneer of *Titanic* and cross-class fantasies of the 1920s are highly conservative attitudes toward class relations. Mr. Cameron concedes a sense of moral superiority to his blue-collar protagonists—but in the end it is the rich who triumph, while the poor return to their "proper" place. Unfortunately, in *Titanic*, that place is at the bottom of the sea: Most of the working-class passengers perish while the rich survive. What sort of triumph is that?
>
> There is a fatalism at work in *Titanic* that suggests this is the way it was and always will be; there is nothing anyone can do to remedy the situation in which the so-called inferior class constantly is oppressed by the superior class. It is this sense of class despair and defeat that makes *Titanic* politically conservative.
>
> Could *Titanic* have been any different? Sure. If working-class people are the betters in the film, then let the rich die and the poor survive. (Ross, "Get Me Rewrite")

Here, the critic has learned the author's view of the class struggle from the outcome of the movie. He need not worry about the argument that in this particular shipwreck the rich did indeed fared better in survival than the poor because the producer of the film could have selected a different shipwreck to dramatize, one in which the rich were duly exterminated. In educational administration and grant-giving, outcomes are in, and the availability of measurable results often determines policy. In literature, the ending offers a great incentive to a critic. By relying on the ending of a text to learn an author's ideology, a critic can save him or herself the trouble of reading the rest of the text.

It is easy to mock a critic floundering for something serious to say about a less than serious film, but first-rate literary minds sometimes use the same method of discovering an author's meaning. Anna Akhmatova attacked Tolstoy for degrading Anna Karenina after she leaves Karenin, because "Tolstoy wished to show that a woman who has abandoned her lawful husband inescapably becomes a prostitute" (Berlin, 195–96). Tolstoy himself reacted favorably to a similar comment by a critic in the 1880s. M. S. Gromeka had called Anna Karenina a passionate woman living for love alone and for it sacrificing family, social position, and finally, life itself. He had claimed that Tolstoy had shown us that in this area (family life), there is no untrammeled freedom; there are laws, and it depends upon an individual's will to follow them and be happy or to break them and be unhappy. Tolstoy praised Gromeka for detecting in a relatively early work the moral positions that Tolstoy propounded in his later writings.

One of these critics attacks Tolstoy and the other praises him, but they agree that his treatment of Anna Karenina's decline and death expresses his view of her deserts. Tolstoy seems to agree with this view in the 1880s, but by then his positions had crystallized in a somewhat different form. In any case, the debate over Anna's behavior seems to inspire real doubts about Tolstoy's skill as a rhetorician. He stated later that an author should infect his readers with the highest moral and religious ideas of his time, and yet good readers cannot agree on Anna's moral status. Gina Kovarsky has offered the best defense of the novel's rhetoric. She argues that there are two kinds of professors: the magisterial one who stands before an audience and propounds the truth, and the dialogic one who sits with the students and stimulates their participation in the exploration of a problem. Usually, Tolstoy was the first kind of professor. We know where he stands. He began *Anna Karenina* with a clear moral position. But as he wrote it, the plot he created led him for a moment into the other style, and he wrote a novel that started a debate that has been educating us for a century and a half.

Though endings do not offer easy moral teachings, the central question here is whether or in what cases we can use the ending of a work of literature to learn the meaning of the work. This approach to the analysis of texts relies on the assumption that the text has a happy ending. Many texts do. In fairy tales, for example, the Ogre tends to come to a bad end, and the nice Hero tends to live happily ever after. Bruno Bettelheim made such endings a part of his definition of a fairy tale and simply excluded unconforming examples from the genre.

> The ending . . . in myths is nearly always tragic, while always happy in fairy tales. For this reason, some of the best-known stories found in collections of fairy tales don't really belong in this category. For example, Hans Christian Andersen's "The Little Match Girl" and "The Steadfast Tin Soldier" are beautiful but extremely sad; they do not convey the feeling of consolation characteristic of fairy tales at the end. Andersen's "The Snow Queen," on the other hand, comes quite close to being a true fairy tale.
>
> (*The Uses of Enchantment*, 37)

Bettelheim's reasoning is not really circular here. He is not describing an existing canon but defining a new one, and the chief threat to his argument comes not from theory but from literary history. Robert Darnton has studied some of these same fairy tales in their eighteenth-century variants, which are often closer to the stories peasants told around the fire than those that Grimm and Andersen collected and presented in nineteenth-century style. Darnton found that endings often are not happy in the earliest versions of the tales he studied. Lévi-Strauss, of course, has denied the true priority of the earliest available version of folk material, asserting that every version adapts the matter of a tale to the social and literary milieu of which it is a part, so that the early version may tell us something about the society, but is just one more version of the tale. Bettelheim's theory gains plausibility if a literary genre is treated as a collection of expectations on the part of the readership. I read many fairy stories to my children when they were small, and once came upon one by Madame d'Aulnoy that ended as follows:

> "Cruel Princess!" said the King, "would you make my life horrible to me by marrying another before my eyes?"
>
> "Not so," replied the Yellow Dwarf; "You are a rival of whom I am too much afraid: you shall not see our marriage." So saying, in spite of Bellissima's tears and cries, he stabbed the King to the heart with the diamond sword.
>
> The poor Princess, seeing her lover lying dead at her feet, could no longer live without him; she sank down by him and died of a broken heart.
>
> So ended these unfortunate lovers, whom not even the Mermaid could help, because all the magic power had been lost with the diamond sword.
>
> As to the wicked Dwarf, he preferred to see the Princess dead rather than married to the King.   (*The Yellow Dwarf*)

My daughters screamed loudly at this outcome, not concerned for the prince (who was a dull stick), nor for the princess (who was a prune), but rather for the genre, the fairy tale as Bettleheim had described it, which demanded poetic justice. They could not have said so, but their literary expectations had been affronted, and Bettelheim was right. This is a genre that small Americans can recognize and respond to, and an important element in its identity is its happy ending. Without this sense on a child's part, there would be no market for the recent children's book about the three little wolves and the big bad pig.

Given that happy endings belong to the collection of stories Bettelheim calls fairy tales, the question remains whether it is proper to assume that *Anna Karenina* has an ending that its author considered happy. For certain genres, such an assumption is justified. In the United States, when talking movies seemed to be as much a threat to public morals as the Internet seems to be today, the film industry tried to set up its own censorship to preempt government intervention. On December 20, 1938, the Hays Office promulgated its "Special Regulations on Crime in Motion Pictures." Certain matters were excluded altogether: "There must be no scenes, at any time, showing law-enforcing officers dying at the hands of criminals. This includes private detectives and guards for banks, motor trucks, etc" (MPAA, in Doherty, 356) Other matters were tightly circumscribed: "With special reference to the crime of kidnapping—or illegal abduction—such stories are acceptable under the code only when the kidnapping or abduction is (a) not the main theme of the story; (b) the person kidnapped is not a child; (c) there are no details of the crime of kidnapping; (d) no profit accrues to the abductors or kidnappers; and (e) where the kidnappers are punished. These last two elements relate to the question of outcomes, which are an important part of many of these regulations: 'no picture shall be . . . approved if based upon the life of . . . a notorious criminal unless the character in the film be punished for crimes shown in the film as committed by him.' "

The reasoning behind such rules can take two forms: Plato had argued that simply seeing a lack of virtue would lead many of us to imitate it; others argue that if crime pays, criminal behavior will become rational. Plato's fear of direct imitation can be justified regardless of punishment. The second of these arguments, however, underlies those Hays Code regulations that relate to retribution and other outcomes. In a movie subject to these rules, it would seem appropriate to explore an author's values by examining which characters get punished. But interpretations of punishment and punishable behavior vary. Preston Sturges's *Miracle of Morgan's Creek* (1944) presented a problem. A character in the movie behaves in a manner that in those times could be called sexually promiscuous, and the Hays Office objected not to her behavior but to the fact that it went unpunished. Sturges replied, in essence, "Not punished? I gave her septuplets!" When literary conduct is constricted by censorship, whether by a government, by commercial considerations, or by political or religious pressure groups, endings, like beginnings, often tend toward the obfuscatory. But when the author plays honestly (or spinelessly) by the rules, it seems fair to expect the ending to reveal the meaning of the work.

In Stalin's time, Socialist Realism included an obligation for "optimism," which normally included a happy ending, although there were a few debates, like the one about the drama *Optimisticheskaia tragediia*

(*The Optimistic Tragedy*). In general, the tragic seems to conflict with the idea of a happy ending. Granted, Aristotle felt that the most successful tragic heroes had a tragic flaw that was in some sense connected with their destruction, but his reasoning is only partly connected with the idea that the flaw itself makes the hero deserve destruction. Aristotle did feel that the destruction of a completely good character would be repugnant to Greek audiences, but this position is very different from the belief that a tragic hero deserves what happens to him. The flaw serves another purpose. Suppose I am walking along the street and a brick falls on my head, killing me. That would be unfortunate for me, but it would not be tragic. To suffer a tragic fate, I would have to be aware of it, struggle against it, and in some sense participate in it. A tragic flaw enables a hero to play a part in his destruction, and without that participation the hero's destruction is not complete. For Aristotle, a thoroughly villainous person's fall from good fortune into misfortune can contain moral satisfaction, but not pity or terror, as the former is for a person undeserving of his misfortune and the latter for a person like ourselves (*Poetics*, 53a3). Aristotle has nothing against moral satisfaction—in fact, he asserts its importance for society in his *Ethics*—but he considers it unrelated to the function of tragedy, which is to produce terror and pity. Fairy tales of the kind Bettelheim describes may be valuable instruments for acculturating the very young to a cruel and confusing world, but they are bad training for reading Sophocles. Oedipus, Ajax, Philoctetes, and the others are great men, and they suffer greatly, but not because they deserve it. Sophocles constructs an ineluctable set of causes, psychological, human, and supernatural, which we sometimes call fate.

The most convincing proof that the moral satisfaction that comes from poetic justice is at most incidental to tragedy is the pair of endings for Euripides's *Iphigenia at Aulis*. In one, the villainous Odysseus triumphs, and Agamemnon takes his nobly obedient daughter from a wedding to the greatest of his warriors and sacrifices her to the otherwise merciless Artemis. In the other version, Iphigenia, like Isaac, is rescued by the divinity, who substitutes an animal. Scholars differ on whether Euripides wrote both versions, but there is no question that both are ancient, which is to say that both satisfied the expectations that ancient audiences held for tragedy. Euripides made Iphigenia undeserving of her fate, but he was working in a genre that permitted but did not demand happy endings.

For novels, the situation is curiously comparable. Critics have attacked Flaubert for killing Emma Bovary at the end of his novel, and called him a prude for punishing her self-delusion and her sexual infidelity. Curiously, we tend not to blame him for rewarding the most thoroughly despicable character in the novel, Homais the apothecary, who receives the Legion of Honor for his attainments. One could perhaps argue that Homais is a comic figure, that poetic justice in comedy is often not for keeps, that there is an old comic tradition in which the villain and the hero end the play by going off to dinner together. But for novels, too, there is some hard evidence that moral satisfaction is simply not a part of the collection of expectations that constitute the genre. Dickens wrote two endings for *Great Expectations*. In one, Pip marries Estella and lives happily with her for a long time. In the other, he lives on in the lonely misery that many readers would say he deserves. Here, the morally satisfying ending collides with the one that gratifies our fondness for the character who has been the center of our attention for hundreds of pages. We readers do not want Pip to get what he deserves. In any case, Dickens proves that the novel does not join the ranks of genres where poetic justice of either kind is built into the genre.

The plots of all great novels and tragedies are about good and evil, but they rarely scold or threaten, and rarely lecture at us. They exercise our moral faculties by forcing us to make decisions and judgments and debate them with the characters and with our peers. The plot can, however, enable us to escape misreadings if it is used intelligently. When I discussed *Dostoevshchina*, I called attention to suffering as a key element. After all, how can one write about Dostoevsky, any more than about *King Lear*, without discussing suffering? Many critics have asserted that Dostoevsky depicted suffering because that was the way he got his kicks. In his 1882 book about Dostoevsky's "cruel talent," N. K. Mikhailovsky expressed this view: "Cruelty and torture always preoccupied Dostoevsky, and did so specifically from the aspect of their attractiveness, from the aspect of the sensual pleasure contained in torturing." Maksim Gorky's 1913 article on Karamazovism (*O 'Karamazovshchine*) made it clear whose pleasure was involved: "Dostoevsky, himself a mighty torturer and a man with a sick conscience, loved to describe just this dark, depraved, antipathetic spirit." The evidence for Dostoevsky's sadism or masochism, however, can virtually always be traced to that insistency in his literary works and occasionally in his conversation which it is adduced to explain. Dostoevsky could be abusive and vicious when he lost his temper, but his documented behavior outside of his writing offers little support for the theory Mikhailovsky and so many others have proclaimed. A second, more prevalent theory claims that, quite apart from any sensations it aroused in him, Dostoevsky idealized suffering—sometimes as a way to Christian salvation, sometimes in order to justify a social system that produced so much suffering, and sometimes for both reasons. Our example of this theory may come from M. A. Antonovich's article on Dostoevsky's "mystico-ascetic novel," *The Brothers Karamazov*, printed in 1881, the year of Dostoevsky's death, a year before Mikhailovsky's article.

> The author so skillfully thought up all the circumstances of the murder that suspicion fell on Mitya, who was altogether innocent. Mitya was arrested and tried. Here emerged all his greatness of soul, all the profundity of his faith and devotion to providence. For the glory of God and for the redemption of his sins, he decided to suffer innocently.... Mitya's decision to suffer innocently in order to be morally resurrected and by this suffering to redeem the suffering of others at first glance seems capricious, the whim of a sick fantasy, and no sort of general moral principle with any serious bases. But in fact, it turns out that this decision is a real moral principle and that it is seriously and passionately preached by such a profound moralist as the elder Zosima, in his teaching, composed, of course, by the author of the novel.
>
> ("Mystiko-asketicheskiy roman")

Antonovich's article has reverberated through Dostoevsky criticism for generations, and I suspect that some of the articles by Russian priests praising Dostoevsky draw their understanding of his novels from Antonovich. He summarizes Mitya Karamazov's position more or less correctly at that moment in the novel, but he ignores the fact that Zosima's disciple, Alyosha, advises Mitya not to take on this suffering, and he represents Zosima's attitude with a major distortion. All three of these critics use a critical technique that we have rejected in this book, the ascription to Dostoevsky of the views of his characters.

The plot of *Crime and Punishment,* like that of *Poor Folk,* however, offers a very different attitude toward suffering. Only a few Dostoevsky characters in these novels appear before and after they suffer. Some, like Razumikhin or Dunya, never suffer. He experiences the pain of cold and hunger, and she the indignity of engagement to Luzhin. But pain and indignity are different from suffering. Pain is the psychological expression of damage to the body, indignity is the same but directed against one's status. Suffering is the psychological expression of damage to the psyche itself. Sonya suffers, but remains unchanged. We see her parents before and after their suffering. Before suffering, her stepmother was a silly provincial girl, most notable for having danced with a shawl before the governor and for marrying a military man for love. After suffering, she is a vicious hag who drags her husband about the room by his hair, beating his head against the floor; drives her stepchild to prostitution and her own children to beg on the streets; spends the tiny sum of money that comes her way on a horrible funeral banquet; and never abates in her ridiculously genteel social pretentions. Before suffering, her husband is an unimportant civil servant so decent that he marries her because he cannot bear to see her and her family starve when she is widowed. Her hectoring and his job loss drive him to drink, destitution, and a cycle of self-inflicted suffering that destroys the lives of those around him. In *Poor Folk,* Varvara risks her life and health caring for her dying parents and the student she adores. She struggles to buy him a gift he longs for, then lets his pathetic father get the credit for it. Then, as we have seen, she suffers in a way we never learn about. After that, she still is kind to the man she loves, but she is not about to starve with him, and she marries a man who had hurt her but can feed her.

The plots of these novels suggest that suffering reduces generosity and kindness and undermines the spiritual and moral worth of these otherwise ordinary people. The most nearly autobiographical of Dostoevsky's major works, *The House of the Dead,* describes his sufferings in a Russian prison camp, but it begins with a rich account of how little penitence or moral improvement such suffering produced.

Despite Antonovich's account, and the word of many separate characters, most of Dostoevsky's plots proclaim that suffering makes us worse people. One great exception to this rule stands out, as we have seen in *Crime and Punishment*. For murderers like Raskolnikov and Svidrigailov, confession, punishment, and suffering can be the only way to salvation.

On issues like suffering, on which critics can have strong impressions, the plot can lead to challenging new readings, but only if we read the text not for poetic justice but for novelistic justice, which is so deeply embedded in the causal system that our childish desires, and those of the characters, cannot prevail against them. At this moment in the history of culture, the powers and the design of verbal plots need special attention, because movies, television, and computer games offer a new set of opportunities to make artistic plots as disruptive as political plots if audiences do not understand the mechanisms of their rhetoric. But that is the beginning of a new story, the story of the gradual transformation of our civilization, its rebirth, and its engagement with a new, hitherto quite unknown reality. This could constitute the plot of a new account—but our present account is completed.

BIBLIOGRAPHY

Aarne, Antti. *The Types of the Folk Tale: A Classification and Bibliography*. Translated and edited by Stith Thompson. Helsinki: Suomalainen Tiedeakatemia, 1928.

Adams, Barry B. *Coming to Know: Recognition and the Complex Plot in Shakespeare*. New York: Peter Lang, 2000.

Alighieri, Dante. *The Divine Comedy*. Translated by Allen Mandelbaum. New York: Bantam Classics, 1982.

The Arabian Nights: Tales of 1,001 Nights. Edited by Robert Irwin. Translated by Malcolm C. Lyons and Ursula Lyons. 3 vols. London: Penguin Classics, 2010.

Antonovich, M. A. "Mystiko-asketicheskiy roman: *Brat'ya Karamazovy*." In *Izbrannye stat'i:Filosofiia, kritika, polemika*, 243–97. Leningrad: Khudozhestvennaya Literatura, 1938.

Aristotle. *Nicomachean Ethics*. Translated by H. Rackham. Cambridge, Mass.: Loeb Classical Library, 1926.

——. *Poetics*. In *Aristotle: Poetics; Longinus: On the Sublime; Demetrius: On Style*, translated by Stephen Haliwell. 1–142. Cambridge, Mass.: Loeb Classical Library, 1995.

Bakhtin, Mikhail M. *The Dialogic Imagination: Four Essays.* Translated by Caryl Emerson and Michael Holquist. Austin: University of Texas Press, 1981.

———. *Voprosy literatury i estetiki.* Moscow: Khudozhestvennaia literatura, 1975.

Barthes, Roland. *S/Z.* Translated by Richard Miller. New York: Hill and Wang, 1974.

Beckett, Samuel. *Waiting for Godot: A Tragicomedy in Two Acts.* New York: Grove Press, 1982.

Bely, Andrei. *Petersburg.* Translated by Robert A. Maguire and John E. Malmstad. Bloomington: Indiana University Press, 1978.

Berlin, Isaiah. "Meetings with Russian Writers in 1945 and 1946," in *Personal Impressions,* edited by Henry Hardy, 198–254. New York: Viking, 1981.

Bessière, Jean, ed. *Passage du temps, ordre de la transition.* Paris: Presses Universitaires de France, 1985.

Bettelheim, Bruno. *The Uses of Enchantment: The Meaning and Importance of Fairy Tales.* New York: Vintage Books, 1976.

Boileau-Despréaux, Nicolas. *The Art of Poetry,* in *The Art of Poetry and Lutrin,* translated by William Soames and John Ozell, 1–65. Oxford: Oneworld Classics, 2008.

Boorman, Stanley C. *Human Conflict in Shakespeare.* London: Routledge and Kegan Paul, 1987.

Boswell, James. *The Life of Samuel Johnson.* New York: Modern Library, 1965.

Borges, Jorge Luis. "Pierre Menard, Author of the *Quixote.*" In *Ficciones,* edited by Anthony Kerrigan and translated by Anthony Bonner, 45–55. New York: Grove Press, 1994.

Bremond, Claude. *Logique du récit.* Paris: Éditions du Seuil, 1973.

Brooke-Rose, Christine. *A Grammar of Metaphor.* London: Secker and Warburg, 1965.

Brooks, Peter. *Reading for the Plot: Design and Intention in Narrative.* New York: Alfred A. Knopf, 1984.

Cardozo, Benjamin N. *The Paradoxes of Legal Science.* New York: Columbia University Press, 1928.

Carroll, Lewis. *Sylvie and Bruno.* London: Macmillan, 1889.

Cervantes, Miguel de. *Don Quixote.* Translated by Edith Grossman. New York: Ecco, 2003.

Chernyshevsky, Nikolai G. "Bednost' ne porok" ["Poverty's no crime"]. In *Polnoe sobraniie sochinenii v piatnadtsati tomakh* 2: 232–40. Moscow: Goslitizdat, 1949.

——. *What Is to Be Done?* Translated by Michael R. Katz. Ithaca: Cornell University Press, 1989.

Chomsky, Noam. *Cartesian Linguistics.* New York: Harper and Row, 1966.

Clarke, Mary Cowden. *The Girlhood of Shakespeare's Heroines: A Series of Fifteen Tales.* New York: AMS Press, 1974.

Comte, Auguste. *The Positive Philosophy of Auguste Comte.* Translated by Harriet Martineau. Kitchener, Ontario: Batoche, 2000.

Continental Airlines. *Sky Mall: The World's In-Flight Shopping Mall.* Holiday issue, 1994.

Cox, Roger L. *Shakespeare's Comic Changes: The Time-lapse Metaphor as Plot Device.* Athens: University of Georgia Press, 1991

Croce, Benedetto. *Essays on Literature and Literary Criticism.* Annotated and translated by M. E. Moss. Albany: State University of New York Press, 1990.

Darnton, Robert. *The Great Cat Massacre and Other Episodes in French Cultural History.* New York: Vintage Books, 1984.

d'Aulnoy, Madame [Marie-Catherine Le Jumel de Barneville]. *The Yellow Dwarf.* In *The Blue Fairy Book,* 38–61. Edited by Andrew Lang. Adapted by Minnie Wright. New York: Longmans, Green, 1948.

Diderot, Denis. *Jacques the Fatalist.* Translated and edited by David Coward. New York: Oxford, 1999.

Dostoevsky, Fyodor M. *Crime and Punishment.* Translated by Richard Pevear and Larissa Volokhonsky. New York: Vintage Classics, 1993.

——. *The Double, and The Gambler.* Translated by Richard Pevear and Larissa Volokhonsky. New York: Vintage Classics, 2007.

——. *Notes from Underground.* Translated by Richard Pevear and Larissa Volokhonsky. New York: Alfred A. Knopf, 1993.

——. *Polnoe sobranie sochinenii v tridtsati tomakh.* 30 vols. Leningrad: Nauka, 1972–1990.

——. *Poor Folk and Other Stories.* Translated by David McDuff. New York: Penguin, 1988.

Egorov, B. F. "Prosteishie semioticheskie sistemy i tipologiia siuzhetov." *Trudy po znakovym systemam* 2 (1965): 106–15.

Eile, Stanislaw. *Swiatopoglad powiesci.* Wrocław, Poland: Zaklad Narodowy im, Ossolinskich, 1973.

Empson, William. *Essays on Shakespeare.* Edited by David Pirie. Cambridge: Cambridge University Press, 1986.

Euripides. *Iphigeneia at Aulis*. Translated by W. S. Merwin and George J. Dimcock. New York: Oxford University Press, 1978.

——. *Iphigenia in Tauris.* In *Euripides II*, translated by Witter Bynner, 117-87. Chicago: University of Chicago Press, 1969.

Fielding, Henry. *Tom Jones*. New York: Random House, 2002.

Forster, E. M. *Aspects of the Novel*. New York: Harcourt, Brace, 1927.

Frankfurt, Harry. *On Bullshit*. Princeton: Princeton University Press, 2005.

Frazer, J. G. *The Golden Bough.* London: Macmillan, 1900.

Freidenberg, Olga M. *Poetika siuzheta i zhanra.* Leningrad: Khudozhestvennaia Literatura, 1936.

——. "Proiskhozhdenie literaturnoi intrigi." *Trudy po znakovym sistemam* 6 (1973): 497-512.

Freud, Sigmund. "Dostoevsky and Parricide." In vol. 21 of *The Standard Edition of the Complete Psychological Works of Sigmund Freud*, translated and edited by James Strachey, 177-94. London: Hogarth Press, 1961.

——. "The Uncanny." In vol. 17 of *The Standard Edition of the Complete Psychological Worksof Sigmund Freud*, translated and edited by James Strachey, 219-52. London: Hogarth Press, 1955.

Frey, James N. *How to Write a Damn Good Novel:A Step-by-Step, No-Nonsense Guide to Dramatic Storytelling*. New York: St. Martin's Press, 1987.

Frye, Northrop. *The Myth of Deliverance: Reflections on Shakespeare's Problem Comedies.* Toronto: University of Toronto Press, 1993.

——. *A Natural Perspective.* New York: Columbia University Press, 1965.

——. *Northrop Frye on Shakespeare.* New Haven: Yale University Press, 1986.

Gei, N. K. *Iskusstvo slova.* Moscow: Nauka, 1967.

Gellrich, Michelle. *Tragedy and Theory: The Problem of Conflict Since Aristotle.* Princeton: Princeton University Press, 1988.

Girandoux, Jean. *Amphitryon 38.* Paris: B. Grasset, 1929.

Girard, René. *Deceit, Desire, and the Novel: Self and Other in Literary Structure.* Baltimore: Johns Hopkins University Press, 1984

Gogol, Nikolai. *The Collected Tales.* Translated by Richard Pevear and Larissa Volokhonsky. New York: Pantheon Books, 1998.

——. *Dead Souls.* Translated by Robert Maguire. London: Penguin, 2004.

——. *The Inspector General.* In vol. 1, *1790-1890*, of *An Anthology of Russian Plays*, translated and edited by F. D. Reeve, 115-29. New York: Vintage Books, 1961.

——. *Polnoe sobranie sochinenii* [*PSS*]. Edited by N. L. Meshcheriakov. 14 volumes. Moscow: Izdatel'stvo Akademii Nauk SSSR, 1937–1952.

Gorky, Maksim. "Eshche o 'Karamazovshchine.'" In vol. 24 of *Sobranie sochinenii v tridtsati tomakh*, 151–57. Moscow: Gosudarstvennoe Izdatel'stvo Khudozhestvennoi Literatury, 1953.

——. "O 'Karamazovshchine." In vol. 24 of *Sobranie sochinenii v tridtsati tomakh*, 146–50. Moscow: Gosudarstvennoe Izdatel'stvo Khudozhestvennoi Literatury, 1953.

Goyanes, Mariano Baquero. *Estructuras de la novela actual*. Barcelona: Editorial Planeta, 1972.

Greimas, Algirdas Julien. *Du sens*. Paris: Éditions du Seuil, 1970.

Gromeka, Mikhail Stepanovich. *Posledniia proizvedeniia grafa L. N. Tolstogo*. Moscow: Izd. N. N. Bakhmeteva, 1884.

Hamilton, Anne. *How to Revise Your Own Stories*. Boston: The Writer, 1946.

Homer. *The Iliad*. Translated by Richard Lattimore. Chicago: University of Chicago Press, 2011.

——. *The Odyssey*. Translated by Richard Lattimore. New York: Perennial, 2007.

Hopkins, Gerard Manley. *The Journals and Papers of Gerard Manley Hopkins*. Edited by Humphrey House. Completed by Graham Storey. London: Oxford University Press, 1959.

Jacobs, Carol. *Telling Time: Lévi-Strauss, Ford, Lessing, Benjamin, de Mann, Wordsworth, Rilke*. Baltimore: Johns Hopkins University Press, 1993.

Jakobson, Roman. "Grammatical Parallelism and its Russian Facet." *Language* 42, no. 2 (April–June 1966): 399–429.

James, Henry. "The Art of Fiction." In *The Future of the Novel: Essays on the Art of Fiction*, edited by Leon Edel, 3–27. New York: Vintage, 1956.

——. *The Art of the Novel*. Edited by R. P. Blackmur. New York: Scribner's, 1934.

——. *The Letters of Henry James*. Vol. 4, *1895–1916*. Edited by Leon Edel. Cambridge, Mass.: Belknap Press of Harvard University Press, 1984.

——. *Roderick Hudson*. Edited by Geoffrey Moore. London: Penguin Classics, 1986.

Johnson, Samuel. *Dictionary of the English Language*. London: J. & P. Knapton, 1755.

Karamzin, Nikolai. *Izbrannye sochineniia v dvukh tomakh*. 2 volumes. Moscow: Khudozhestvennaia Literatura, 1964.

——. *Selected Prose*. Translated by Harry M. Nebel Jr. Evanston, Ill.: Northwestern University Press, 1969.

Kayser, Wolfgang. *Das Sprachliche Kunstwerk*. Bern: Francke, 1967.

Keats, John. "La Belle Dame Sans Merci." In *Complete Poems*, edited by Jack Stillinger, 270–71. Cambridge, Mass.: Harvard University Press, 1982.

Kermode, Frank. *The Genesis of Secrecy: On the Interpretation of Narrative*. Cambridge, Mass.: Harvard University Press, 1979.

——. *The Sense of an Ending: Studies in the Theory of Fiction*. New York: Oxford University Press, 1967.

Kipling, Rudyard. *Just So Stories*. Mattituck, N.Y.: American House, 1976.

Kovarsky, Gina. "Rhetoric, Metapoesis, and Moral Instruction in Tolstoy's Fiction: *Childhood, Boyhood, Youth*; *War and Peace*; and *Anna Karenina*." Ph.D. diss., Columbia University, 1998.

Lamb, Charles, and Mary Lamb. *Tales from Shakespeare*. London: J. M. Dent & Sons, 1921.

Lermontov, Mikhail. *A Hero of Our Time*. Translated by Vladimir Nabokov and Dmitri Nabokov. Garden City, N.Y.: Doubleday, 1958.

Leskov, Nikolai. *The Enchanted Wanderer*. Translated by David Magarshack. New York: Modern Library, 2003.

Lessing, Gotthold Ephraim. *Laocoön: An Essay Upon the Limits of Painting and Poetry*. Mineola, N.Y.: Dover, 2005.

Lévi-Strauss, Claude. *Tristes tropiques*. New York: Penguin Books, 1992.

Levitan, L. C., and L. M. Tsilevich. *Siuzhet v khudozhestvennoi sisteme literaturnogo proizvedeniia*. Riga, Latvia: Zinatne, 1990.

Lotman, Jurij M. *Stat'i po tipologii kul'tury*. Vol. 1 of *Materialy k kursu teorii literatury*. Tartu, Estonia: Tartuskii Gosudarstvennyi Universitet, 1970.

Makkai, Adam, ed. and trans. *Toward a Theory of Context in Linguistics and Literature: Proceedings of a Conference of the Kelemen Mikes Hungarian Cultural Society, Maastricht, September 21–25, 1971*. The Hague: Mouton, 1976.

Meijer, Jan. "Situation Rhyme in a Novel of Dostoevsky." In *Dutch Contributions to the Fourth International Congress of Slavicists*, edited by Carl L. Ebeling, 115–29. The Hague: Mouton, 1958.

Meijer, Jan M., and Jan van der Eng. *The Brothers Karamazov by F. M. Dostoevskij: Essays*. The Hague: Mouton, 1971.

Meletinsky, E. M. *Paleoaziatskii mifologicheskii epos*. Moscow: Nauka, 1979.

Mikhailovsky, N. K. *Dostoevsky: A Cruel Talent*. Translated by Spencer Cadmus. Ann Arbor, Mich.: Ardis, 1978.

Milton, John. *Paradise Lost*. New York: Oxford University Press, 2004.

Miracle of Morgan's Creek. Directed by Preston Sturges. Hollywood, Calif.: Paramount Pictures, 1944. Film.

Molnár, Ferenc. *The Play's the Thing: A Comedy in Three Acts*. Adapted by P. G. Wodehouse. New York: French, 1927.

Montague Browne, Anthony. *Long Sunset: Memoirs of Churchill's Last Private Secretary*. London: Cassell, 1995.

Montaigne, Michel de. "On Experience." In *The Complete Essays*, translated and edited by M. A. Screech, 1207–70. London: Penguin, 2004.

Morson, Gary Saul. *Narrative and Freedom: The Shadows of Time*. New Haven: Yale University Press, 1994.

Motion Picture Association of America [MPAA]. "Special Regulations on Crime in Motion Pictures" (1938). Full text can be found in Thomas Doherty, *Hollywood's Censor: Joseph I. Breen and the Production Code Administration*, 355–56. New York: Columbia University Press, 2007.

Nashe, Thomas. "Litany in Time of Plague." Originally published as a song in "A Pleasant Comedie, called Summers' Last Will and Testament," in vol. 3 of *The Works of Thomas Nashe*, edited by Ronald B. McKerrow, 282–84. Oxford: Basil Blackwell, 1958.

Nekliudov, S. "Staticheskiie i dinamicheskie nachala v prostranstvenno-vremennoi organizatsii povestvovatel'nogo fol'klora." In *Tipologicheskiie issledovaniia po fol'klor*, 182–90. Moscow: Nauka, 1975.

Nietzsche, Friedrich. "The Will to Power as Art." In *The Will to Power*, edited by Walter Kaufmann, translated by Walter Kaufmann and R. J. Hollingdale, 419–53. New York: Vintage, 1968.

Opochinin, Evgeny N. "Besedy s Dostoevskim" ("Conversations with Dostoevsky"). In vol. 6 of *Zven'ia*, edited by L. P. Grossman, 457–84. Moscow: Academia, 1936.

Ostrovsky, Alexander N. *Poverty's No Crime*. In *Plays by Alexander Ostrovsky*, translated and edited by George Rapall Noyes, 67–133. New York: Scribner, 1917.

Parish, Charles. *CliffsNotes on Sterne's "Tristram Shandy."* Lincoln, Neb.: Cliff's Notes, 1968.

Pasternak, Boris. *Doctor Zhivago*. Translated by Richard Pevear and Larissa Volokhonsky. New York: Pantheon Books, 2010.

Petrovsky, M. A. "Morfologia novelly." In vol. 1 of *Ars Poetica*, edited by M. A. Petrovsky, 69–100. Moscow: Gosudarstvennia Akademia

Khudozhestvennykh Nauk, 1927. http://dbs.rub.de/gachn/files/ Ars_poetica_vip_1.pdf.

Plato. *The Republic.* Cambridge, Mass.: Loeb Classical Library, 1963.

Plautus, Titus Maccius. *The Brothers Menaechmus [Menaechmi].* Translated by Palmer Bovis. In vol. 4 of *The Comedies,* edited by David Slavitt and Palmer Bovis, 79–174. Baltimore: Johns Hopkins University Press, 1995.

Poe, Edgar Allan. *The Narrative of Arthur Gordon Pym of Nantucket.* New York: Penguin, 1999.

Polti, Georges. *The Thirty-Six Dramatic Situations.* Translated by Lucille Ray. Boston: The Writer, 1977.

Porter, Cole. *The Complete Lyrics of Cole Porter.* New York: Alfred A. Knopf, 1983.

Prince, Gerald. *A Grammar of Stories.* The Hague: Mouton, 1973.

Propp, Vladimir. *Istoricheskie korni volshebnoi skazki.* Leningrad: Izdatel'stvo Leningradskogo Universiteta, 1946.

——. *Morphology of the Folktale.* Translated by Laurence Scott. Austin: University of Texas Press, 1968.

Pushkin, Alexander. *The Complete Prose Tales of Alexandr Sergeyevich Pushkin.* Translated by Gillon R. Aitken. New York: Norton, 1966.

——. *Eugene Onegin: A Novel in Verse.* Translated by James E. Falen. Carbondale, Ill.: Southern Illinois University Press, 1990.

——. *Polnoe sobranie sochinenii.* Edited by V. D. Bonch-Bruevich and Maksim Gorky. 17 vols. Leningrad, 1937–1959.

——. "The Tales of the Late Ivan Petrovitch Belkin." In *The Complete Prose Tales of Alexandr Sergeyevich Pushkin,* translated by Gillon R. Aitken, 61–140. New York: Norton, 1966

Rabelais, François. *Gargantua.* Edited by Pierre Michel. Paris: Gallimard, 1973.

——. *Gargantua and Pantagruel.* Translated and edited by M. A. Screech. London: Penguin Books, 2006.

Reyfman, Irina. *Ritualized Violence Russian Style: The Duel in Russian Culture and Literature.* Stanford: Stanford University Press, 1999.

Ricoeur, Paul. *Time and Narrative.* 3 vols. Translated by Kathleen McLaughlin and David Pellauer. Chicago: University of Chicago Press, 1984–1988.

Ross, Steven J. "Get Me Rewrite: Class Fatalism Pervades Old-Fashioned *Titanic.*" *Los Angeles Times,* January 4, 1998. http://articles.latimes.com/ 1998/jan/04/opinion/op-4819.

Saussure, Ferdinand de. *Writings in General Linguistics*. London: Oxford University Press, 2006.

Scragg, Leah. *Shakespeare's Mouldy Tales: Recurrent Plot Motifs in Shakespearean Drama*. London: Longman, 1992.

Shakespeare, William. *The Complete Works of Shakespeare*. Edited by G. L. Kittredge. Boston: Ginn, 1936.

Shcheglov, Yuri, and Alexander Zholkovsky. *Generating the Literary Text*. Translated by L. M. O'Toole. Oxford: Holdan Books, 1975.

Shklovsky, Viktor. *Razvertyvaniie siuzheta*. Letchworth, U.K.: Prideaux Press, 1979.

——. *Theory of Prose*. Translated by Benjamin Sher. Elmwood Park, Ill.: Dalkey Archive Press, 1991.

Shore, Rima. "Scrivener Fiction: The Copyist and His Craft in Nineteenth-Century Fiction." Ph.D. diss., Columbia University, 1980.

Shvarts, Evgeny. *Klad* [The treasure]. In vol 1. Of *Sobranie sochinenii v 5-i tomakh*, 72-127. Moscow: Knizhnyi Klub Knigovek, 2010.

Sidney, Philip. *Sir Philip Sidney's Defense of Poesy*. Edited by Lewis Soens. Lincoln: University of Nebraska Press, 1970.

Simmons, Ernest J. *Dostoevsky: The Making of a Novelist*. New York: Vintage, 1962.

Sophocles. *Oedipus at Colonus*. Translated by Robert Fitzgerald. In *Sophocles I: Antigone, Oedipus the King, Oedipus at Colonus*, edited by David Grene and Richmond Lattimore, 77-157. 2nd ed. Chicago: University of Chicago Press, 1991.

——. *Oedipus the King*. Translated by David Grene. In *Sophocles I: Antigone, Oedipus the King, Oedipus at Colonus*, edited by David Grene and Richmond Lattimore, 9-76. 2nd ed. Chicago: University of Chicago Press, 1991.

——. *Philoctetes*. Translated by David Grene. In *Sophocles II: Ajax, The Women of Trachis, Electra, Philoctetes, The Trackers*, edited by David Grene and Richmond Lattimore, 189-254. Chicago: University of Chicago Press, 1969.

Spenser, Edmund. *The Faerie Queene*. Edited by Thomas P. Roche and C. Patrick O'Donnell. London: Penguin Books, 1979.

Stanzel, Franz K. *Theorie des Erzählens*. Göttingen: Vandenhoeck und Ruprecht, 1979.

Stendhal [Marie-Henri Beyle]. *Racine and Shakespeare*. Translated by Guy Daniels. New York: Crowell-Collier Press, 1962.

——. "Racine et Shakespeare." In vol. 16 of *Oeuvres completes*, edited by Georges Eudes. Paris: Pierre Larrive, 1953.

Sterne, Lawrence. *The Life and Opinions of Tristram Shandy, Gentleman*. London: G. Allen and Unwin, 1985.

The Storming of the Winter Palace. Directed by Nikolai Evreinov. USSR, 1920.

Swift, Jonathan. *A Tale of a Tub*. In *A Tale of a Tub and Other Works*, edited by Angus Ross and David Woolley, 1–103. New York: Oxford University Press, 1986.

Tate, Nahum. *The History of King Lear, a Tragedy: As It Is Now Acted at the King's Theatres*. London, 1759.

Thompson, Stith. *Motif-index of Folk-Literature: A Classification of Narrative Elements in Folktales, Ballads, Myths, Fables, Mediaeval Romances, Exempla, Fabliaux, Jest-books, and Local Legends*. 6 vols. Bloomington: Indiana University Press, 1955–1958.

Todorov, Tzvetan. *Grammaire du Decameron*. The Hague: Mouton, 1969.

Tomashevsky, Boris. *Teoriia literatury: Poetika*. Leningrad: Gosudarstvennoe Izdatel'stvo, 1928.

The True Chronicle History of King Leir and His Three Daughters, Gonorill, and Cordella. London, 1605.

Tsilevich, L. M., ed. *Siuzhet i khudozhestvennaia sistema*. Daugavpils, Latvia: Daugavpilskii Pedagogicheskii Institut, 1983.

Tsvirkunov, V. *Siuzhet: Deiaki pytanii teorii*. Kiev: Vyd-vo Akademii Nauk URSR, 1963.

Tolstoy, Leo. *Anna Karenina*. Translated by Richard Pevear and Larissa Volokhonsky. New York: Penguin, 2000.

——. *Polnoe sobranie sochinenii v 90 tomakh* [*PSS*]. Moscow: Khudoszhestvennaia Literatura, 1950.

——. *What Is Art?* Translated by Aylmer Maude. Indianapolis: Hackett, 1996.

Vaiman, S. "Vokrug siuzheta." *Voprosy literatury* 2 (1980): 114–34.

Veselovsky, Alexander. *Istoricheskaia poetika*. Leningrad: Khudozhestvennaia Literatura, 1940.

Virta, Nikolai. *Sobranie sochinenii v 4-kh tomakh*. 4 vols. Moscow: Khudozhestvennaia Literatura, 1980–82.

Vogüé, Melchior de. *The Russian Novel*. Translated by H. A. Sawyer. New York: Doran, 1914.

Voprosy siuzheta i kompozitsii. Edited by G. V. Moskvichev. Gorky: Gor'kovskii Gosudarstvennyi Universitet, 1974, 1976, 1978, 1980.

Voprosy siuzhetoslozheniia: sbornik statei. Edited by L. M. Tsilevich. Riga, Latvia: Zvaigzne, 1969, 1972, 1974, 1976, 1978.

Walpole, Horace. *The Castle of Otranto.* New York: Dover, 1966.

Webster, John. *The White Devil.* In *The Duchess of Malfi and Other Plays,* edited by René Weis, 1–101. New York: Oxford University Press, 1996.

Wilson, Robert. *The Life and Times of Joseph Stalin: An Opera.* Music composed by Alan Lloyd and Igor Demjen. Performed on December 21, 1973 at the Brooklyn Academy of Music. Brooklyn, New York: Robert Wilson Audio/Visual Collection, 1973. DVD (24 discs), 1,454 min.

Wright, Austin M. *The Formal Principle in the Novel.* Ithaca: Cornell University Press, 1982.

Wurzbach, Natascha. *The Novel in Letters: Epistolary Fiction in the Early English Novel.* Coral Gables: University of Miami Press, 1969.

Zhanr i kompozitsiia literaturnogo proizvedeniia: mezhvuzovskii sbornik. Kaliningrad: Kaliningradskii Gosudarstvennyi Universitet, 1974, 1976.

Zola, Émile. *The Experimental Novel and Other Essays.* Translated by Belle M. Sherman. New York: Haskell House, 1964.

——. *Le roman expérimentale.* Paris: Charpentier, 1923.

INDEX

diction, 3, 26, 27, 43, 44, 45

Diderot, Denis, 46

dispositio, use of term, 17

Disraeli, Benjamin, 66

disruption, use of, xv, 53

Divine Comedy (Dante), 20

Don Quixote (Cervantes), xx, 25, 26, 38, 83, 91

Dostoevshchina, xv, 108, 136

Dostoevsky, Fyodor: as anchored in Russian tradition that preceded him, xxii; *The Arabian Nights* and *Don Quixote* as recycled in fiction of, xx; as challenging current literary leaders by reinventing psychological plot, 96–100; coincidences in works of (*see* coincidences); compared to Freud, 99; as deeply Christian, 114; desire in works of, 110, 112; distaste for spiritualism by, 120; evolution of plotting in fiction of, 85; favorite authors of, 102; gentry as practically unrepresented in works of, 111; as having made many mistakes, 116; impact of Gogol on, 93; importance of causation to, 89–90; letter novels as offering resources that matched literary needs of, 84; as mocking great and little scientific minds for operating not on reason but on faith, 120; one-sidedness of desire and violence in *Crime and Punishment* as more peculiar to plotting of than the *Dostoevsh-china*, 108–14; parallelism in works of, 103; parallel structures of desire and violence in works of, 112, 114; plot of *Crime and Punishment* as reflecting background of in history of literature as well as own evolution as novelist, 101; Razumikhin as Dostoevsky character most like, 60; as shaped by Russian version of nineteenth-century novel, xv, 86–95; situational rhyme in novels by, 28; on suffering, 136–37, 139; use of epilogue by, 122; use of epistolary form by, xxii; as wild man, 84. *See also specific works*

Double, The (Dostoevsky), 98, 99

dramatic irony, xiv, 18, 56

dramatic plots, 43, 45, 47, 54, 112

dramatic romance, 58

"Dream of a Ridiculous Man, The" (Dostoevsky), 123

eavesdropping, 89, 104, 115

Eisenstein, Sergei, 20

Emin, Fyodor, 92

emotions (of audience), 45, 46, 48, 53, 90

Empson, William, 75–76

Enchanted Wanderer, The (Leskov), 22

English comedies, tragedies, and sonnets, Shakespeare as creating central canon for, 58

epic plots, 43, 82

epics: as differing from dramas, 79; fabula and siuzhet in, 17;

WORKS BY ROBERT L. BELKNAP

Belknap, Robert L. *The Genesis of "The Brothers Karamazov."* Evanston, Ill.: Northwestern University Press, 1992. Translated into the Russian by L. Vysotsky as *Genezis "Brat'ev Karamazovykh"* (St. Petersburg: Akademicheskii Proekt, 2003).

——, ed. *Russianness: Studies on a Nation's Identity: In Honor of Rufus Mathewson, 1918–1978.* Ann Arbor, Mich.: Ardis, 1990.

——. *The Structure of "The Brothers Karamazov."* Evanston, Ill.: Northwestern University Press, 1989. First published 1967 by Mouton. Translated into the Russian by Vadim Baevsky, et. al., as *Struktura "Brat'ev Karamazovykh"* (St. Petersburg: Akademicheskii Proekt, 1993).

Belknap, Robert, and Richard Kuhns. *Tradition and Innovation: General Education and the Reintegration of the University.* New York: Columbia University Press, 1977.